THE

PRUNING BOOK

Major portions of this book and most of the illustrations were first published by Rodale Press in 1948.

The
PRUNING BOOK

By

GUSTAVE L. WITTROCK

Former Custodian of Herbarium
The New York Botanical Garden

Illustrations by
Doris Clark

Edited and with an Introduction by
MAURICE FRANZ
Managing Editor, Organic Gardening & Farming

RODALE PRESS, INC.   BOOK DIVISION
Emmaus, Pa. 18049

Standard Book Number 0-87857-008-X
Library of Congress Catalog Card Number 73-172066
Copyright 1971 by Rodale Press, Inc.
Printed in the United States

OB-561
Fifth Printing — August 1975

CONTENTS

[v]

INTRODUCTION

by Maurice Franz, Managing Editor
Organic Gardening & Farming Magazine

WE TAKE great pleasure and pride in once again making available—after a lapse of 20 years—this fine gardening reference work which belongs in every homesteader's library. It was first published in 1948, went through three printings in as many years, and was then permitted to drop off into undeserved neglect.

In bringing it once again to the attention of the gardening public, we have reshuffled the order of the chapters in an effort to regroup them according to kindred interests and probable frequence of reference. But the work itself remains unchanged and durable, just as Gustave Wittrock wrote it more than a quarter of a century ago. And we have taken particular care and pleasure to include here in pristine form his preface to the original edition.

Let it be said here at the outset that, just as in gardening, there are no pruning "secrets"—only good practice and habits. More than anything we want this work to be a common-sense gardening book, one that you will take into your hand when you have a job to do, and then use just as you would any gardening tool.

So, once again with pride and pleasure, we ask you immediately to turn to page 153 where our "Pruning Guide for 225 Woody Ornamentals" begins. We think you will learn to use this Guide before you plant, when you plant, and later, when you are training your trees and shrubs. As the late Dorothy Franz once said: "If a home planting has been wisely planned, pruning ornamentals is a minor job."

We'll take that advice and try to build on it here as a cornerstone. If this book helps keep your pruning chores minor, it's done its job well and has earned its place in your library. Use it wisely and often in the planning and operation of your home grounds—we've designed it to give you a happy homestead.

And now it remains to discuss briefly the three great questions of Why? When? and How? which must be asked —and should be answered—at the outset of all human activity, gardening and otherwise.

Why do we prune?

When is the best time to prune?

And, finally, how do we prune correctly?

These are the questions that should be discussed briefly and intimately here and now. They are also the questions to whose investigation and correct response Gustave Wittrock dedicated his life.

WHY DO WE PRUNE?

Essentially we remove part of a tree, a shrub, or a flowering plant to help nature. There has been damage, or the plant is growing badly and is interfering with its own development. Sucker growths in the crotches of established limbs do no good except to rob the plant of part of its vitality and should be removed—the thumbnail seems to have been designed for just this purpose.

In addition to repairs, tree and shrub pruning is necessary to balance the top and the roots, to change or control the size and shape of the plant and to regulate the number or development of flowers or fruits. We suggest extra-careful attention to Chapter 9 on Roots and Root Pruning if you are working with transplanted trees. Rootlets are always left in the soil when a tree is dug, and more damage further reduces the number of working, vital roots. So, since your new tree can't possibly supply its original number of. branches in its new site, be prepared to cut away much of the top growth—as much as half—to bring it into realistic balance with the reduced root system.

This is the proper time and place to investigate the nature of plant growth because we will find that successful pruning practices ultimately depend on an understanding of its principles. There are two kinds of growth tissue—primary and secondary. Primary growth or meristematic tissue consists of specialized plant cells—my Webster's dictionary says they are "capable of dividing indefinitely"—that are found at the tips of roots or in buds at the tips and on the sides of branches.

The buds at the tips of the branches—the terminal buds—are usually the most active. They can be relied on to make the annual spring growth of a shrub or tree. The topmost terminal buds, plus a tree's main upright stem, is called the leader. *If the topmost terminal bud is removed or injured, the first lateral bud behind it will go into action and*

[ix]

become the leader. This rule also holds good for the terminal buds on side branches.

Secondary growth tissue is the layer of cells called the cambium tissue which lies between the bark and the woody center of a branch, trunk or root. As many of us know from our studies in plant photosynthesis, it transports raw materials for carbohydrate manufacture to the leaves from the roots, and carries back again sugars and starches to the roots. Also, the cambium helps produce both the woody tissue and the tree's bark. Finally, and highly important to the pruner, all wounds are healed by the growth process originating in the cambium layer which is responsible for the annual increased thickness of the tree trunks, branches and roots.

The theory of pruning is based on these two growth factors which occur in buds and the cambium. For instance, many gardeners make their plants bushier by pinching out the soft tissue at the end of a branch—again, the thumbnail seems to be designed for just this purpose. But, how does it work? Although you've pinched off the terminal buds, the roots and stem are still delivering just as much sap to the branch as they did when the terminal bud was there, growing and using the sap. So the extra sap now forces its way into one or more of the lateral buds which also contain meristematic tissue and are waiting for the chance to grow. You've given them just that with a little judicious thumbnailing, and each lateral bud that is forced into growth develops into a new, elongating branch.

But every time you pinch back a plant, there is a pause in the growth pattern, while readjustment takes place. If two new branches form after a pinching operation, it is easy to understand that they will make less growth than the single one that was removed because, for the time being,

[x]

they are still getting only as much sap as was consumed by the single branch.

If, after pruning, only a single branch continues to grow instead of the two you expected, the plant will be smaller than it would have been unpinched. *This same result will follow any type of pruning.* Every time you prune a plant during its growing season, you remove some of the food-manufacturing equipment in its leaves—again, see photosynthesis. And each reduction in food output correspondingly reduces the size of the mature plant, even though the setback is temporary. So the effect of all pruning is to dwarf the plant.

Flowers that profit from pinching include chrysanthemums, asters, cosmos, marigolds, annual candytuft, snapdragons, heliotrope, petunias and zinnias. If you want to produce unusually large flowers for show purposes, try disbudding, that is, pinching out the side buds instead of the terminal buds. All the growth then goes into the terminal bud, and the flower it produces is a very large one. Disbudding is most often practiced to produce large chrysanthemums, dahlias or roses. The terminal buds of some flowers should never be pinched back because that is where they bear their spikes of blossoms. This group includes columbine, delphiniums, foxglove, gladiolus, hollyhocks, poppies and tulips.

If the flowers of the daisy family are pinched back partially—half the stems in a clump—the flowering period will start sooner and last later. This practice also applies to gaillardias and phlox.

WHEN IS THE BEST TIME TO PRUNE?

"Whenever your knife is sharp." That's how Dr. William H. Eyster said it in his Introduction to the 1951 edition of this book. As we will see when we consult the "Pruning Guide" on pages 153-170, our pruning knives (also the thumbnail!) should be sharp for almost 12 months of the year. There is always some plant on the home ground that will benefit from your thoughtful and observant attention.

Shade trees should be pruned once every three or four years to keep the tops open. Summer or early autumn is the best time for pruning birches, elms and maples while flowering trees may be pruned as soon as they have finished blooming—generally in the spring. The spruce and fir may be pruned late in March or late in June without injury. Junipers, cedars and arborvitae may be cut any time, preferably from April to mid-August. Pines are pruned with the best results late in June or early in July. Pruning can be done with the fingers, breaking off the growth "candle" about midway on each shoot. Spruce may need two prunings to keep them small enough for the sites assigned them. The first pruning is done in the early spring, before growth started, when half of last year's growth is cut back. The second pruning, done later in the spring or in the summer, nips out the tips of the new growth in the same way that the pine "candles" are pinched back.

In general, trees may be pruned at any time of the year, P. P. Pirone advises in *Tree Maintenance*. Common sense observation also tells us that pruning for shape is best done when the trees are in full foliage—it is easier to see dead or weakened branches.

Most trees are best pruned in the early spring because most rapid healing of wounds will occur then. But some, like the maples and birches, "bleed" so profusely when cut in the early spring that it is better to delay pruning until summer when the sap runs more slowly.

INTRODUCTION

The evergreens usually do not need the periodic pruning you give the deciduous trees. The main object in pruning evergreens is appearance—to produce a more bushy or compact plant. Pruning the ends or tips of the branches literally forces the plant to make new *inside* growth, along the branches. Not all evergreens can be pruned identically or at the same time—the methods employed depend upon the type and species. For a fuller report check the Pruning Guide for woody ornamentals, also Chapter 8 on the Culture and Pruning of Evergreens.

HOW TO PRUNE

Since that is what Gustave Wittrock's book is all about, this is the place to speak only in generalities which serve to cite the excellent and plain-spoken text. If you must trim evergreens, here are a few rules worth following:

1. Leave the lower limbs on the tree as long as they are alive and healthy. Maybe they get in the way of the mower, but those lower branches help to make the evergreen's typical shape, and should not be removed.

2. Avoid drastic pruning in the late summer or autumn. Removing outside limbs exposes the weaker inside branches that, unaccustomed to exposure, will be subject to winter damage when outer protection is taken away.

3. Avoid pruning beyond or past live foliage. Evergreens do not readily put out new growth when cut down to the old wood.

4. Prune yearly, but lightly.

5. When leaders fail to develop or are broken, particularly in pines and spruces, bend the nearest shoot into the position the leader would occupy, and tie it in place with a stake to brace it. After one or two months, remove the

[xiii]

stake and pinch off any small shoots that may be competing for the leader's position.

The broadleaf evergreens—rhodedendrons, American holly, evergreen, barberry, laurel and many of the tropicals —call for less pruning than the narrow leaf evergreens. Sometimes, the broadleaf species may be cut back after blooming when they are too straggly. But they should be cut back to another green shoot or an active bud. Bear in mind, once again, that evergreens do not put forth new growth from old wood too readily.

But here the inner voice tells us that our time is up and that we are infringing on the grounds of the down-to-earth, practical text. May your pruning knife ever be sharp! And—don't make any cuts without thinking, "Will it help the plant?" And be sure to make full use of the Pruning Guide for 225 Woody Ornamentals that starts on page 153.

MAURICE FRANZ

PREFACE
to the Original Edition

THIS book has been written as a service to the amateur who desires to learn how to care for his own plantings. The information recorded is based primarily on records of my own practical experience in pruning. Observation of trees I trimmed 20 years ago in Illinois has been most instructive; even the mistakes have become practical information. Work on fruit trees and berry bushes in California and Washington has also contributed to my knowledge.

How many, during emergencies, have discovered how little they knew about the proper care of fruit bearing plants. The average individual had the confidence to attempt the care, but, in most cases realized that he lacked the knowledge. You have met these people; it may have been your own experience. An attempt has been made to give "hints," to help the amateur to solve problems in pruning, presented in simple and graphic terms with illustrations so that the principle of pruning can be readily understood.

There are really no trade secrets in pruning. No tree or shrub can hide the results of pruning; the plant's reaction to the "clipping" is ever present; the amateur needs only to observe. I have often taken groups out to a tree or into an orchard and called attention to neglect or to the response of the tree to pruning. The whole history of the tree's life and its care can be practically read by noting the old wounds, and how they healed, what would have happened had the branch survived, and, what the tree may have been like in shape and form had nothing been done. One can learn a great deal basically about pruning by simply observing the results of past work on trees and shrubs, irrespective as to how many years ago the pruning has been done.

Pruning culture is as old as civilization. New experimental knowledge on the growth process of plants has not altered the basic principles of pruning culture. This book, hence, is for the practical amateur desiring the basic knowledge of pruning. My hope, in writing the book, has been to stimulate a better appreciation of our shrubs and trees and to make one conscious of the fact that these living things, plants of nature, are really a part of our environment. If these living plants are neglected they influence our mental attitude; pruned, trimmed, cleaned and dressed, our plants make for a happier outlook and a reward in better fruit, handsomer trees, and a gratifying pride in observing our gracefully flowering shrubs.

G. L. WITTROCK.

Chapter One

SELF-PRUNING AND ITS ADVANTAGES

HOW DO PLANTS GROW?

A PRUNER MUST UNDERSTAND the process of growth before he attempts pruning. If he snips and cuts at random without knowledge of the basic principles of the growth-process, he may innocently injure the plant, and it is this fact that causes many authorities to hesitate advising an amateur to prune his own stock. One often observes the pruner's lack of proper knowledge of the plant simply by watching his work and the result of his effort. If he understood how a plant grew, he would be more hesitant in cutting a limb or a branch; he would prune logically and with forethought.

The tissue that is the seat of new growth is called meristematic tissue. This new growth is either primary or secondary. Primary meristematic tissue is found on the extremes of the plant; in the aerial part of the plant it is located in the buds, either terminal or lateral; and in the subterranean part of the plant it is found at the ends or tips of the roots. The bud encloses this embryonic growing tissue. Thus, the bud is the seat of the growing point for height or elongation of the plant, and is spoken of as a protective enclosure of primary meristematic tissue. The bud may remain dormant for months or it may never burst forth into active growth, unless it should be necessary to continue the growth of the plant. Millions of lateral buds remain dormant in an average tree, but nature has this form of preparedness ever ready to assure growth, should replacement of leaves, branches, and stems be necessary. Terminal buds are normally the most active in most species and are apt to continue growth when the growing period is favorable. But if this terminal bud is injured, killed by frost, or if it is faulty in some way, the immediate lateral bud will be stimulated to carry on and become the leader. Thus, when pruning, one must recognize these delicate areas and remember that by cutting back, active terminal buds are severed. Dormant lateral buds must then carry on the function of elongating the branch; in young trees, care should be taken not to cut through the lateral bud or to it, since this leads to direct exposure. If too long a stub is left above the bud, the stub is also subject to drying up and decaying, thus injuring the bud. The ideal cut is ⅛ to ¼ of an inch above the bud, which then has a chance to survive.

The other primary growing tissue of the plant is at the terminal points of the tiny, delicate rootlets. This colony of primary meristematic cells is the original parent of all the cells that make up the spreading, elongating, basic net-work of the root-system. The rootlet is constantly pushing forward, reaching for soil salts and water to supply the aerial part of the plant. These rootlets are very important and must be understood by the pruner, particularly when he is transplanting and pruning the roots before setting the plant into a new location. This will be discussed under root pruning. Thus, the root-tip and the bud are the meristematic growth centers of a plant, and they account for the elongation of a plant in height and the spreading out of the root-system. Growth in width is accomplished by secondary meristematic tissue and usually appears after the primary tissues of twigs and roots have matured.

Secondary growing tissue is found between the bark and wood of roots, twigs, branchlets, stems, and trunks of the plant. This tissue is called the cambium layer, and consists of a thin, slimy layer of minute brick-shaped cells. These microscopic cells are almost rectangular in outline, thin-walled and easily torn, especially during the growing season. The function of the cambium layer is to produce and increase the diameter of the stem, branch, limb, root or trunk, and to heal wounds. All secondary wood and bark originates from this active growing layer or cylinder of living, dividing cells. If a limb or stem is girded by a wire, the wire will eventually strangle the cambium layer and kill the branch or tree. Any injury to this important layer is always serious; a sliding ladder placed on a branch may strip, crush, or bruise the protective bark and injure the cambium, especially in the springtime when it is active. Spiked shoes used in climbing may puncture the bark to the cambium layer and cause the slimy, sweetish, living substance to ooze out and attract insects and fungi, since this substance is the cream of nutritious food. Both the insects and the fungi will feed on this ooze, thus penetrating the injured bark tissue and establishing a foothold within the plant. A struggle will

[3]

ensue between the plant, which is trying to heal the injury, and the insect or fungus.

WHAT IS MEANT BY PRUNING?

Cutting out dead wood is only a phase of pruning. The purpose of pruning is to remove the excess, handicaps, the struggle of part with part, thus increasing the chance of a plant to gain better growth, greater strength, and the maximum production of flowers and fruits. It is also in part a process to shape a plant into a definite form. There are usually more branches on a plant, on its sides or in its crown, than can possibly survive; a large proportion will die through the struggle for existence. Nature eliminates and selects by a slow process; controlled pruning does this quickly and thus may be defined essentially as a thinning process.

WHY DOES ONE PRUNE?

When one thinks of the millions of neglected trees and shrubs that make up the flora of our natural forests and waysides he may well ask the question: "Why prune a plant?" These plants survive, they bear flowers and fruits; they have apparently done this for eons, long before man came to this earth and thought of pruning, so why prune? If these plants live, reproduce, all pruning technique appears superfluous. We speak and think of these native trees and the shrubs of a natural forest and the open country as "wild" and uncontrolled. Some explorers report on their expeditions that they had "to push and struggle, forcing and cutting a path through untamed, scrambling masses of undergrowth of a primeval forest." We may answer our question "Why prune?" with these words: "We prune to civilize and tame plants and to bring them under control to our advantage, to aid the plants and shrubs in producing better fruit and flowers, and finally to give longer life to the plants." Pruning has been practiced since the dawn of civilization, particularly for fruit culture. To many, the idea of pruning is only notional and they challenge its value; others resort to extreme pruning, heading in, dwarfing, and selecting. There is, however, a form of pruning practiced by nature that we usually fail to realize and recognize.

PRUNING HELPS NATURE

Were we to give nature a hand in the forests, help remove some of the crowding caused by seedlings, reduce the struggle for existence, remove badly diseased trees to pre-

Long-handled pruning shears are essential for "topping".

vent further contagion and even take off the lower dead branches that were the results of accidents or shading, we would certainly increase the life cycle of the selected forest trees. This type of care is the function of forestry—the study of protecting, selecting, and preserving our natural forests. We in America have been rather thoughtless of this type of care since we are still rich in natural forests. The Department of Agriculture is, however, beginning to realize that our wealth in timber is diminishing. Forest care is really being considered seriously, as it has been for centuries in the Old World. Promiscuous slashing and lumbering is now discouraged; it will soon become illegal. And man in America is learning that, to keep his forest perpetuating, he must give nature a hand, he must prune.

NATURE PRUNES ITS NATIVE TREES

Nature's method of pruning may be considered as haphazard, inefficient, reckless, or destructive, but there is a natural process that can be observed readily by simply walking through a virgin or neglected forest. In fact, nature is the best teacher of the basic principles of pruning, if we but take time to observe. Branches that are weak, die; crossing or rubbing branches kill each other; branches that develop at an angle too obtuse from the trunk are weak and eventually have little chance to survive, particularly when loaded with the weight of their own fruit; they snap off. And if the tree lags in growth, its young seedlings will soon telescope through the lateral branches, surpass the parent tree and shade it out of existence. Dead limbs and branches and even dead trees are not "sawed off" by nature, but the good old friend, the wind, as it blows through the forests and sweeps the land, acts as the pruner, snaps off all the dead and weak material. This is a natural phenomenon and

[6]

can easily be observed. It is, however, a slow process and certainly must be classed as most haphazard since the branches have to be fairly well rotted before the wind can snap them off, unless the wind is a high gale; then green branches go too. Even this destructive gale reveals basic principles of pruning.

Walk through a wood after a high wind or an ice storm and note the damage; you will readily observe why some green branches snapped, and others survived. One does not have to be an exceptional detective to learn how nature prunes. The first clue to observe is the terrible struggle for existence in a plant or forest association; undershrubs struggle for a bit of sunlight that may escape through the trees above, and even the trees among themselves are fighting to hold their place in the forests against the crowding of seedlings and younger and more vigorous growth pushing up from below. Even the prairies with their matted sod condition hem in the forests or try to do so. This narrow strip between a forest and prairie association is spoken of as "No-plants-land" by ecologists. There one may observe the plant battle: the forest trees attempting to push ever forward, but their seeds usually fail to penetrate the matted sod. If they succeed to germinate they may fail to survive the crowded conditions and the bright sunlight. While the prairie plants are ever disbursing their seeds by many methods into the forest, the seedlings, if they germinate, may fail to grow because of the forest shade.

The trees within the forest group bear their dead branches for long periods, awaiting the wind to prune them off. While these dead branches are still on the trees and shrubs, a second factor of destruction enters, the scourge of fungi and insects. These dead branches are the pastures for parasitic and saprophytic fungi, since the limbs no

[7]

longer have their protective barks, containing cork cells and various chemicals such as tannin to protect against such invasions. And many of these parasites, followed by boring insects, will pass through the decay and enter healthy wood. Thus a forest tree is rarely in perfect health, handicapped as it is by dead branches, fungi, insects, and crowding; naturally in many cases the life span of the plant is shortened. On the other hand, one is impressed by the vitality of a tree, struggling on though badly injured or diseased, and with all the handicaps of dead branches in excess, still having sufficient vitality to shoot out new, strong, vigorous branches, twisting these upward to become a new trunk and carry on the life of the tree.

DOES PRUNING INJURE PLANTS?

Does cutting off limbs and branches injure the tree or plant? What is the physiological response of a plant to pruning? Pruning, if practiced with the correct knowledge, common sense, good sharp tools and a bit of muscular effort, is a benefit, whether on an herb, shrub, or tree. We have observed that pruning is a natural process in the woods. You now may ask, is it harmful or devitalizing to the plant? Pruning is not a devitalizing process; it is harmful only when the wounds made by pruning do not heal quickly and disease sets in. The notion that pruning is harmful arises from the false analogy with animals that suffer shock or injury when parts are removed. The reasoning follows: a tree is a living organism, therefore, it too is shocked by the removal of parts. The fact is that a tree or a plant is not that kind of an organism and in no sense can it be compared with animals in reference to this type of treatment.

Let us return to the woods again after a severe storm.

[8]

Thin Wood Pruning—Cross Section

Have you ever noticed the crown of a tree twisted off, leaving almost a naked trunk with hardly any lateral branches left? Watch the response of this tree during the season and during the following years. You may even notice trees that underwent such mishaps 4 to 6 years previously. They have survived in most cases. You must have observed avenue trees topped back to 6-inch wood with the laterals also cut severely. Did they die? A group of mulberry trees near my home was topped back to 8-inch wood three years ago. This spring I noticed the new growth now crowning the top with copious branches radiating from the center 10 feet long. A row of poplars near a railroad station was topped four years ago, 15 trees in all. The apparently severe pruning was not harmful. Only one consequence has been observed; flowers and fruits have not developed to date. Apparently the growth, arising from adventitious buds and acting like sucker-growth, must attain a certain proper age for fertility, the length of time depending on the species.

This loss of temporary fertility is implied in the general warning on the harms of excess pruning. Of course, wounds caused naturally, biotically, or by careless pruning are always subject to resultant consequences if they do not heal. But the actual pruning apparently did not "shock" the trees. In fact, experiments have not revealed the limits of pruning. For example, one recent scientific experiment used tomato roots to prove that osmosis was based on root pressure. The stem was removed from the crown of the plant and the root stem was inserted in a glass tube and sealed. The roots were then placed in a solution of water with nutrients, the objective being to note how high the roots could osmotically push up a column of water. These roots were kept alive for weeks for the experiments, and just how long they would have lived or if they could have formed a bud is not known. Conversely, we prune off shoots, set them in sand as a practical method of propagation. These cuttings not only survive, but develop new roots, and in time spring forth into a complete plant with flowers and fruit. We may conclude without hesitation that pruning is not harmful if practiced judiciously.

PRUNING VITALIZES PLANTS

We have referred to the woods with the definite purpose of observing the existing competition and the struggle for existence among plant life. If we remove some of this competition, remove some of the competitors, and become partial to a few plants, giving them ample room, our selection will indeed respond remarkably, and the vitalization will be easily observed. This is also true with branches of a tree. We must interpret a tree as a community, composed of buds, leaves, twigs, branches, rootlets, and roots. All these are comparable to a modern city with competitive industries and with a division of different kinds of specialized labor. Within its own sphere, there is competition, either success or bankruptcy, but always a battle to survive.

Each leaf is individually struggling against its neighbor, striving for the best seat by twisting, elongating its petiole, and poking its competitor out of position by excess growth or greater mechanical strength, aided also by its position on the twig of which it is a part. If the twig is at proper angles from the branches and if it succeeds against other twigs of the same branch, the little leaf we spoke of at first has that much more chance. And even the branch has its problem of competition—it too must struggle against crowding with other branches. This is not all; the branch may have the best of positions as far as the top of the tree is concerned, but it must compete for the water supply from

[11]

the root system. If we remove all this excess waste of competition and permit the energy, so expended, to be diverted into growth and production, the response is rejuvenation; the process of doing it is pruning. We must now study the complexity of a plant to understand the basic value of pruning.

Chapter Two

CORRECTIVE PRUNING

KNOWING HOW PLANTS grow in height and how the roots spread out as they radiate from the tree into all directions, and also realizing that living tissue is always present under the bark of either roots or stems to increase thickness of the plant, we can now discuss a few facts about pruning that must be generally observed. The act of pruning always causes wounds. Unfortunately, it is a necessary evil. These wounds by the pruner may be so small as to pass unnoticed. A pruner may consider a small wound as most insignificant, particularly when he is using a hand clipper or a pole shear or pole saw. Some scoff at the seriousness of a wound if it is less than one inch in diameter, and only if the wound is on the trunk of a tree, is there any concern; shrub wounds are ignored entirely. The fact is that whether a wound is 1 foot across or $\frac{1}{100}$ of an inch, it becomes a sore spot in the plant, and until thoroughly healed, it is constantly sub-

[13]

jected to fungi. The open tissue is a constant invitation to fungi to take possesion; through these wounds, ranging from minute to large, they penetrate the branches and trunks of trees. Fungi spores float in the atmosphere; they are always present. When they alight on healthy bark they fail to germinate, but if by chance they should come in contact with an unprotected wound, an opening into the internal structure of the plant, they vegetate and by rapid development bring on a diseased condition. An injured leaf or a bruised fruit is also the target of a barrage of fungi spores from the air, hungry for this sort of opening to start their work of destruction.

PRUNING TOO MUCH

The work of a pruner must be conducted with the minimum amount of bark or skin injury. As stated before, he must not climb trees with spiked or hob-nailed shoes; he should wear rubber soles, tennis shoes preferably, since the rubber soles will not slip on wet bark or injure it. He must not slide ladders carelessly on branches, but place them carefully, and if extended high, rope them on the limb as a safety measure. If he uses ropes on the tree, he should be sure that his anchor rope is securely tied on healthy bark and that it will not slide too seriously.

No tree or shrub should be pruned until the operator knows why he is pruning. He should diagnose his tree, note the dead and injured limbs and branches first, and then decide what additional healthy branches should be removed, if balance is necessary, or if the green limbs removed are going to be a serious handicap for the health of the tree. No branch should be removed until a good reason for doing so has been concluded and an observation has been made as to the influence and effect of such a removal. This leads us

[14]

to a second rule: not more than 2 or 3 large healthy branches should be removed in one season, especially from large trees. Observation shows that our greatest fault in pruning is not that we prune too much, but that we prune too much at one time. Inordinate pruning at one time not only makes many unsightly scars and exposes too many areas to fungi, but it induces a great deal of suckers to develop, a normal reaction when pruning is on the excess side.

RESPONSE TO CUTTING OFF BRANCHES

One form of injury to a tree in removing a healthy branch is the quantity of leaves that are thus lost to the tree. This rule varies proportionally with the age of the tree and the kind of species being treated. The older the tree, the greater is the possible injury; and a slow growing species is obviously more handicapped than one that is normally a fast growing tree. The principle effect of cutting off a part of a plant, particularly during the dormant season, is to increase the vegetative vigor of the parts remaining, since there is more available stored food to tap. It means an increased amount of water and other supplies. This increase of available food for growth does not, however, mean that the plant as a whole will become larger, though its leaders may increase. Pruning, in general, is a dwarfing process because of the reduction of leaf surface; the less leaves there are, the greater the decrease of prepared food.

HOW TO CUT A LIMB

There is only one way to cut a branch from a tree, and that is to cut it the safest and surest way for the remaining scar to heal. One is not interested in the cut limb, but he is concerned about the tree from which it is cut. The proper cut is not the easiest one. The shortest cut through a limb is

[15]

at right angles to its diameter, as illustrated in the figure at "D," but this will leave a stump even though one may start the cut at the crotch of the trunk at "E." (See page 17.) This stump is a hindrance to the healing of the wound. Indifference to the health and appearance of the tree is the reason for which one so often observes stumps left on shade, ornamental, or fruit trees. Let us examine what actually happens to a stump left on a trunk. Sap will not flow out into a stump 6 inches long, as a general rule; thus there will be no healing. If the stump is shorter, *some* healing can be expected. If the stump is less than one inch long, complete healing or a considerable amount of it can be anticipated. Suppose the stump is 1 inch long from the trunk, how will it heal?

What could happen in the meantime while the healing is going on? As we have learned, it is the cambium layer or secondary meristematic tissue that increases the thickness of a trunk or limb. How long will it take the trunk to increase in diameter to cover the 1 inch stump? Species vary in their growth in thickness, but let us assume that the average annual increase of a trunk is $\frac{1}{16}$ of an inch. To reach the end of the stump it would require 16 years, and then one must add another 5 years for the cambium layer to fold over the stump, since a 4 inch scar requires 6 years to heal. Thus 21 years are required, more or less, providing the stump remains healthy. During these 21 years the stump is subjected to fungi, bacterial rot, and boring insects. If attacked, the stump dies back and may rot into the tree long before the tree can heal or outgrow the stump. If the decay is faster than the healing process, a cavity results, which in its constant rotting process will eventually become so large that the tree is doomed, because any cavity is a weakening factor, both from the point of view of health and

[16]

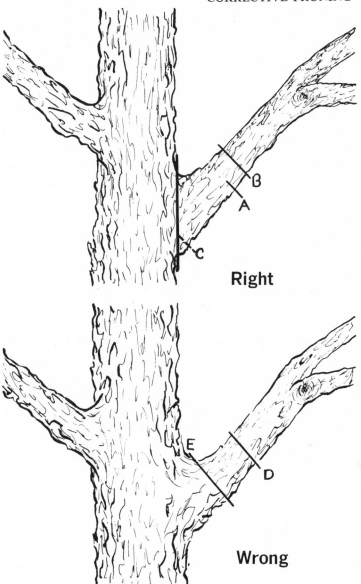

Right

Wrong

Right and Wrong Way to Cut a Limb.

mechanical strength; a strong wind can and does snap the tree at this weak point. On the other hand, should the tree succeed in healing the stump before the rot penetrates, the stump within the tree becomes the knot hole of timber. Knot holes in forest trees, particularly if they are partly decayed, fall out and make a poor grade of timber. The condition and the quantity of knot holes determine the grade of lumber. Let us return to the proper cut of a limb.

The proper cut of a limb should be parallel to the trunk of a tree. This rule applies to all trees in general, whether shade, ornamental, timber, or fruit trees. This cut may result in the largest one in terms of diameter, but it will be the easiest and best cut to heal. If the limb is more than 2 inches thick, 3 cuts should be made. The first cut is the under-cut, from 6 inches to 1 foot from the trunk of the tree, as shown in the illustration at "A." (See page 17.) Then the upper-cut at "B," a few inches further out on the limb from the under-cut, is the next step; this cut is made through the limb or until the branch snaps off by its own weight. By this method there will be no tearing of the bark which is one of the serious consequences of pruning. Tearing the bark of the trunk is equally as serious as leaving a stump, because the injury is not always so easily detected, but water, insects, and spores of fungi can find the condition readily. After the weight of the limb has been removed by the preliminary cutting, the final cut of the remaining stump at "C" is made. If the stump is thick and heavy, from 4 to more inches in diameter, a careful pruner will make a 4th cut on the underside of the stump at the point where the final cut will come through; this is done to break through the bark and to ensure against ripping. Or the pruner may tie up the stump to prevent it from falling and tearing the bark when the final cut is made. Once the saw is through, the stump will hang suspended on the rope, which then can be released and the piece lowered to the ground. I have observed many accidents at this point of the operation, where the careless pruner failed to use proper precautions; when he cut off the stump it would not only tear the bark of the trunk, but would fall off, hit his ladder and knock it out from under him, or crush his foot on the rung of the ladder and bruise him in general. Precautions may seem exaggerated, but they must be observed in removing limbs to ensure safety and the best chance for a tree to survive.

A. The under-cut from 6 to 12 inches from the main cut.

B. The upper-cut 1 to 2 inches from "A."

C. The final cut.

D. The cut one should never make because it leaves a stump.

E. The cut that some advocate as the smallest cut, close to the trunk. In this cut, however, there is still a stump from "E" to "C" which would require years to heal. This type of stump is most conducive to the formation of adventitious buds or suckers which are devitalizing and wasteful of food supplies.

TYPES OF GREEN BRANCHES CLASSED AS WEAK

In the general form of a tree, many branches develop that are destined to die within a few years because of their location, their mode of attachment to other branches, and their relation to the general form of the tree. These branches are the ones selected by a pruner to thin out a tree, particularly in the case of fruit trees. These weak branches are sucker growth or water sprouts, horizontal forks of equal thickness, and under-branches of a main branch. All of these types of branches should be removed because they are

[19]

The first cut, or undercut, on a limb should be made from 6 inches to 1 foot from the tree's trunk.

harmful and weak, and endanger the tree. If a tree has been properly trained when young, these types of branches will not be present, but often a neglected tree has them and they reveal the neglect. To describe these types in detail let us first consider the sucker types.

The sucker types of branches usually arise within the tree from adventitious buds. These buds develop spontaneously, usually near wounds, but they can arise from normal bark, particularly if the tree has been pruned and cut severely. They grow very fast the first year, are soft and flexible and do not cause serious harm at first, but if they remain for the second and third year or more, they thicken in diameter, become stiffer and rub other branches, bruising them as they poke through to the top of the tree seeking light, thus opening the bark of the older limbs and exposing them to fungi. The age of the sucker growth reveals the number of years a tree has been neglected. An abandoned fruit orchard is an illustration. Often these suckers arise from below a grafted tree, and since the stock of the graft is usually selected because of its hardiness and vigor, the sucker will have just that much more vitality. And if sucker growth does not completely kill the limbs of the grafted material by rubbing, it will crowd them out by the principle of the survival of the stronger in natural competition.

The second type of a weak branch is the fork. This is illustrated in the following figure. The fork type splits readily in a heavy wind or if one branch of the fork has more fruit than the other; thus, a fork, when loaded, will split away. It is the one type of branching that a pruner must guard against while standing in a tree. If he is within the heart of the tree, pruning the crown, he must never trust standing on a limb of a fork, even though it may be 3 to 4

[21]

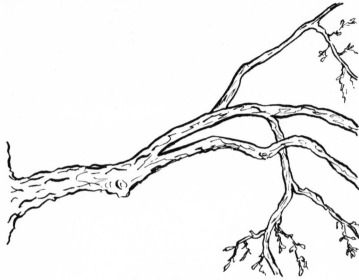

Fork Branch

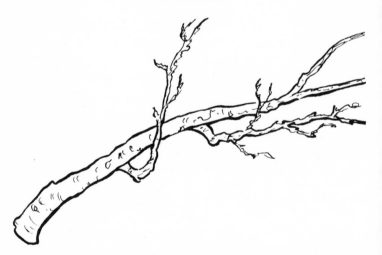

Under Branches

Weak Branches

inches in diameter. I have observed many accidents in trees because of this carelessness on the part of a pruner. If not too severe, it is best always to remove one of the limbs. Should it, however, make too big a hole in the form of the tree, it is best to resort to braces a few feet from the fork, with bolts firmly screwed through the center of each limb, but always with the objective that someday one of the limbs will be removed. I have personally experienced standing on poplars, with the limbs of the fork 4 inches in diameter—they shredded off almost as paper, they were so weak.

All of the above factors apply equally to the third type of weak branch, the under-branch. Often they appear in the primary development of the tree, and at first are not serious because of their flexibility, but as they grow older and become a part of the framework of the tree, they are the weaker branches. They also develop from a sucker origin, the adventitious bud arising from the underside of an older limb. The young sucker growth either elongates horizontally to an opening in the crown of a tree, or twists around the limb to grow upward or vertically toward the top of a tree.

CLIMATIC CONDITIONS VS. PRUNING

There is a close relationship between climate and pruning, a factor all pruners must recognize. It is possible to remove more branches of a plant under wet climatic conditions than under dry. An exposed tree, isolated to dry winds and exposed to the sun, cannot adjust easily to severe pruning. If its trunk is pruned too high, the soil below it is exposed and dries out quickly. Lower lateral branches shade the base of the tree and umbrella the immediate soil. Oak trees are very sensitive to exposure and loss of protective shade. Thinning out or topping the crown of a tree also reduces shade. Not only does shade serve as a nursery for delicate plants, but it also conserves the moisture of the immediate soil surrounding the plant. It is a simple test to note the lower temperature and higher humidity under the shade of a tree compared to that immediately away from the shade of a tree; the shade of the plant makes up part of its climatic environment. We are often advised: let there be air for proper circulation under a plant. But too much air circulation acts as a dryer and an evaporator of needed moisture.

Thus, we may conclude that a tree is greatly influenced by the conditions of environment, such as light, the quality of the soil, whether heavy or light, the amount of water and air retained by the soil, the character of the subsoil, and the general climatic conditions of the region, particularly the amount of rainfall. It is necessary to know how the plant responds to these various factors; this can be learned by studying the plants, the trees, and the weeds within the area. Good common or judicial sense and observation are all that is necessary.

Chapter Three

AN APPROACH TO
TOP PRUNING

AN ISOLATED tree in an open field may have a short thick trunk and a spreading top; the same species in a forest or growing with other trees in a colony becomes tall with a slender trunk and a narrow top. Trees on high, cold mountain sides and dry plains are generally low and spreading. These types are natural responses to the environmental conditions, especially light and wind. Pruning can alter a great deal of this natural form. If one checks terminal branches, he induces the development of laterals, thus developing a spreading tree; conversely, after removing the laterals and pruning the sides severely, the response is in the height of the tree. If we desire high trees with high crowns we simply prune the laterals from the trunk from time to time as the tree grows, and thus we prevent the formation of low crotches. In the case of wind brakes and screens, low, stocky trees are best, planted close together; very little pruning is

[25]

necessary other than removing dead or broken limbs and cutting back the top terminals and leaders. Whether trees are grown for timber, cultivated for fruit, for shade or artistic purposes, each desired result requires a specific treatment. Topping and cutting out loose and straggling habits in trees may turn them into shapely specimens. Deformities may be overcome easily by pruning and free growing trees may be transformed into dense hedges or into artificial shapes. Never clip the head of a young tree to resemble a squared hedge.

"Topping" fruit trees is thought to induce greater fruit-bud production.

[26]

Topping is most resorted to in the care of fruit trees, for the following reasons:

1. High fruit trees necessitate climbing; thus there is always the danger of limbs breaking or high winds snapping off the higher branches.

2. Low trees can be more easily shaped and controlled.

3. The crop can be harvested better from low trees than from high ones.

4. Fungi and insects are more easily controlled.

5. Since the greatest vigor of a tree is near the top, topping spreads this vigor to other parts of the plant; thus the height vigor is harnessed.

6. A low tree is less drain on the soil fertility; food value of compost is not lost in unnecessary height.

7. Trees close to the ground protect against drought of the soil; shade over the immediate soil conserves the natural soil moisture.

8. In topping, it is wise to remember that a few well developed branches are of more value than many which are crowded together cutting off the light and air. This crowding is often the result of excess topping; thus, one must check the condition throughout the season.

TIME OF PRUNING

The question, "When is the best time to prune a fruit tree or to trim trees in general?" is often asked. The average man shrugs his shoulders with, "Whenever I have the time." This time seems to be for most people in the spring, in the fall, even during the winter months, but rarely during the summer. By many authorities summer pruning is considered as pruning at the wrong period, in spite of the fact that it

[27]

is the best period of the year for most types of trees in general, and particularly for many varieties of fruit trees. The general practice is to prune trees in the early spring, when the urge to get outdoors is so tempting. The soil may be too wet to work; thus, the only thing to do is to clean up the grounds and trim the shrubs and trees, cutting out the dead branches and the "winterkill," and to prune in general. No thought is apparently given by some as to whether this period, spring, is the best time for plants or as to how the tree may respond to the spring shearing.

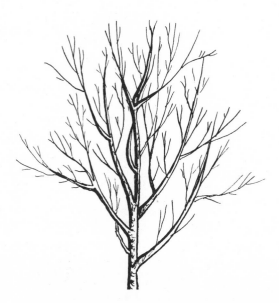

Peach tree at planting time.

[28]

WINTER PRUNING

Let us first discuss seasonal pruning, starting with the winter months. What is the general response of the tree when trimmed during the cold dormant period of winter? The slogan, "If you want wood, prune in the winter," is often quoted of authorities. First, all one can do is to cut out dead branches and summer injury, but this does not include possible "winterkill" because it cannot be anticipated nor detected until the sap begins to flow in early spring. The more severe the cutting, the greater will be the sucker

Same tree pruned.

[29]

growth in the spring and more wood will be produced at the expense of flower and fruit production. This is a natural response. Not only will many dormant buds open in the spring that would normally not swell and burst open, but adventitious buds will develop from the bark tissue, particularly on branches that have been cut back or "topped." The greatest accumulation of food and growth activity concentrates at the ends of branches; if they have been cut back or topped, the ends of stubbed branches become most active with development of adventitious buds. Secondly, winter is not a comfortable time in which to prune because of the cold, the danger of slipping on icy branches, and because of the brittle nature of the branches. During winter healthy limbs may snap easily under the weight of a pruner, resulting in the possible loss of important branches. We must also realize that branches and limbs do not freeze during winter, in spite of the suggestion made by one authority who states that "Winter pruning has its advantage since wood is frozen and will cut easily." If the contents of a limb, or "wood," is frozen, that part of the limb dies.

Plants are divided into oil, fat, or sugar trees: the oil and fat trees are usually most dominant in temperate and arctic regions, whereas sugar trees are found further south, from the temperate regions to the tropics. When the winter season starts, the sap of the trees is concentrated into fats, oils, or sugars, a slow physiological reaction to temperature brought on through the fall period. This concentration of the sap reduces its freezing point. It is parallel in principle to that of putting honey, molasses or "anti-freeze" liquids into the radiators of our cars to reduce the freezing point of the necessary fluid of the car. Thus, in the winter time, plant sap is concentrated and remains stored within all parts of the plant, protecting the living protoplasm from freezing.

[30]

This living substance, as we have learned, is ever present, immediately under the bark of stems and roots and in the buds. The concentration of fats, oils, or sugars permits trees to survive temperatures of 50 degrees below zero and lower. It is surprising to note the low temperatures recorded near the timber line in the arctic circles, or as one finds them near the tops of lofty mountains. If the limbs are injured, if the cold temperature can penetrate through the layer of cork cells, through the concentrated sap, and freeze out the water from the "hibernating," though living protoplasm, the living substance dies; it cannot revive with thawing. That is why small branches die back most readily; they have so little protection compared to the thick branches. This is also well illustrated in the rose shoots and grape canes; often the ends of the shoots are killed back, particularly during a severe winter.

Conversely, "winterkill" is also often the result of an early thaw, for instance in February, when a warm spell suddenly breaks a cold winter siege. The sap of the tree cannot adjust so quickly to this raised temperature. The concentrated sap is almost without water; the soil surrounding the tree is still gripped in frost varying from 4 to 18 inches and deeper, and so the roots cannot become active. Yet transpiration will start with the balmy thaw; the result is a drought condition. Limbs die for the want of water, and we refer to these limbs as "winterkilled." Consequently one would have to prune a second time and to consider a great portion of the winter pruning as superfluous and wasted effort. The action of sudden freezing of immature and imperfectly ripened wood in the fall or early spring is also an opening for disease. That apparently incurable malady in plants known as "yellows" is thought to start with sap that has become contaminated at frozen points, the prompt removal of which will often prevent the spread of the disease.

Some authorities advocate pruning in February or early March before sap begins to flow. The wound does tend to dry and is not apt to "bleed" and waste its vital food sap. This is possible with some plants like grapes and roses and many species of shrubs.

Winter is, therefore, not advocated as the best pruning season unless one desires a preponderance of "wood" growth, as described by horticulturists, since by "wood" they mean vegetative growth, and by fruit they mean flower bud production. But wood production is always a response to heavy pruning and this can be induced equally well by pruning in the fall.

FALL PRUNING

Pruning trees in the fall season has some advantages over winter pruning because of the comforts of the milder season. But what in general can one really prune during this season? Summer injury should be taken care of immediately, and there should be very little sucker growth left to be removed in the fall. Winterkill cannot be anticipated, so why not simply leave the plants alone during this period? If some of the slender branches are to die by freezing back during the winter period, why not plan accordingly and permit excess summer growth to remain and let it become the injured material during the winter months? It can be removed the next season, whereas, if removed in the fall, more branches may die back, and their removal may then be serious and a handicap to the tree.

However, one fact must be disclosed about fall pruning that some consider of value. The buds that are retained on a plant after fall pruning will benefit by the accumulated nutriment stored in the plant, which would otherwise have been distributed over a greater number of buds. They have thus a more vigorous start in the spring, advance more rapidly in growth during the summer, and their maturity will naturally be hastened, a condition of great importance in some districts and regions where the summer seasons are rather limited. This type of pruning, however, is followed by a big "if"; that is, if the remaining shoots and buds survive winter and do not suffer winterkill.

We have learned that transplanting is best performed during the fall season when the leaves have fallen, when transpiration is at a minimum and when the injured roots of the plant will have a chance to repair for the next season. But if one must cut out excessively from the transplanted plant, one must recall the rule that the removal of large amounts of wood brings on excess growth of laterals and thus produces much vegetative wood, whereas by cutting back slightly, fruit or flower buds are stimulated the following season. Let us watch the following season, the response of a few trees that have been pruned in the fall and winter; this observation will be the best teacher.

Let us assume that we have under observation a group of trees pruned early in the past season. Spring is here and buds are swelling and bursting, the roots are active and, if they have not been disturbed or pruned, they are assimilating water osmotically and pushing it ever upward into the trunk, the shoots, and to the very tips of the buds. If the plant has been pruned and topped and is out of balance, there will be more water present than necessary, and the fats, oils, sugars, and starches will have been reconverted to available food, which is also circulated ever upward. If pruning has been in excess, what will become of this extra food? Growth activity is at its height; the nourishing sap

[33]

concentrates at the extremities. If these extremities are cut-back wounds, cortical cells in this region immediately above the cambium layer begin to divide; sometimes in the hundreds, and these divisions divide again and again. Soon the excess nourishment has an outlet, this being newly formed adventitious buds and the shoots that come from them. This is the ever present consequence of excess pruning in the fall, winter, and early spring.

SPRING PRUNING

Most people prune in the spring. In early spring the sap begins to flow and growth activity is at its height. Without question, this is the worst time to prune. The sap may ooze out of the wound and this valuable nutritive food may become sour and spoil by bacteria. The decay of sap causes rot around the exposed wound. True, one can remove all "winterkill," bad branches, and injuries of the previous summer and winter, but the tree's response to the pruning is in the production of excess sucker growth as already described. We know the consequence of suckers, how they sometimes are almost parasitic in their greedy drain on the stored food supply. It takes a great deal of food for a sucker to grow as quickly as it does.

During the spring period one might prepare the soil around the plant and aerate it by cultivation. There is one form of pruning that can be done in mid-spring; that is to check, by pinching back, the active development of new wood growth—inducing growth of flowers and fruit. The converse is also true—by checking the growth of flowers the vegetative growth will be stimulated. This sometimes is desired, if the plant is young or weak and wood growth is necessary. The most active and vigorous parts of a plant are naturally the ones which will have access to the most

[34]

nourishment; otherwise they would not be vigorous. While these parts are making active growth other parts will grow more slowly. Late spring pruning has a decided influence in retarding early summer growth.

EARLY SUMMER PRUNING

Why not prune in the summer months? During this period, growth is well established and pruning will not bring on excess sucker growth. Cutting back at this time induces fruit buds to develop in greater proportion to wood buds. In fruit trees, in late June or early July, after the flowers have set and small fruit is already visible, cut out excessive green branches if weak, even those with fruit on them, since reducing the amount of fruit gives the remaining fruit a better chance to grow on strong branches. All the excessive potential growth left after pruning the tree will be diverted from making suckers, and will be used to increase the size of the fruit and even accentuate its taste.

There are, however, many diverse opinions on summer pruning. Some authorities actually discourage pruning at this time. They claim that the loss of the leaves is too serious and that it does not repay for the effort thus expended. Others say it is detrimental and dangerous for the health of the tree. Yet from June to July, the leaves are well developed, the elaborate sap accumulation of the tree has been largely used in the formation of new wood, which is at its peak of growth in August. Because of this fact, healing of a wound may be expected to be visible in a week or 10 days, if trees are pruned in June or July: this has been my observation during years of experience as a tree surgeon. I consider it a protective measure to prune at this time since apparent healing in August can always be more or less expected. The value of this is that the growth activity has

[35]

sealed the bark to the wound, protecting it through the non-growing season of the fall and winter until spring, when vigorous growth resumes. We have already discussed the value of pinching back and disbudding during the seasons, particularly in the summer. The response is definitely toward fruit-bud formation instead of wood. We must now add a word on protection of large wounds that have been made on trees.

PRUNING BY PINCHING-BACK AND DISBUDDING

The wise pruner does not wait for limbs to grow out and then saw them off annually; he prunes by pinching out the terminal buds. This is a very simple process which requires very little exertion. A robust shoot can be checked at an early stage by pinching out its terminal growing point. Thus, growth in length is checked without the removal of foliage, while the growth vigor of the shoot is diverted to other buds and shoots develop where a more active extension is required. This technique is much practiced with berry and fruit trees. Disbudding is the technique of removing a bud or young shoot that has not made more than one inch of growth. This is practical pruning, since weak growth is removed at an early stage, and its removal is absolutely harmless to the plant. This is a practical method of preventing growth where it is not wanted. The pinching-back and disbudding methods are the most rational modes of directing the growth of plants. These types of pruning are started early in the season and carried on throughout the growing period; by this method there will be little need for winter pruning or removal of branches, whether small or large, unless they are diseased or broken by storms and winds. Rubbing off a bud in May saves cutting off a branch in December. With this type of pruning, however, it is assumed that the plants have been prepared properly at transplanting time, or in the case of neglected plants, that they have had proper basic pruning. One may class this type of pruning as weekly inspection over an orchard throughout the season, and particularly as summer pruning.

PROTECTION OF WOUNDS

There are many compounds on the market that are excellent preservatives of wounds; these I recommend. On the other hand, coal tar, though it may be used, is often injurious to the cambium, especially of fruit trees; heating the coal tar before applying drives off some of the more volatile materials that are really harmful. Creosote mixtures are often used as a disinfectant; white lead paints are also used, with the idea that the oil in the paint will prevent the entrance of water and the white lead may kill insects chewing through it. If some wounds are very large they should be painted every year as a precaution, since very large wounds sometimes take many years to heal. Some trees bleed in the growing season, such as elms and maples, and thus loosen the plant covering; these too should be painted every year.

Tools you need include pole saw and clipper, pruning saw and shears.

Chapter Four

FLOWER-BEARING PLANTS

FLOWER-BEARING HABITS OF FRUIT PLANTS

A PRUNER must know the flower-bearing habits of a fruit-bearing plant before he can prune intelligently for fruit. The location of the development of flower buds is determined by the kind of variety, the age, and the vigor of the plant and the quantity of the food supply. Hybrid varieties develop many exceptions and rarely conform to the general flower-bearing habits of the original parent species. The development of fruit buds may be divided into the same 2 classes as given for flowering shrubs, in the case of which the flowers are borne on the season's growth of new wood, or from the previous year's wood. Learning these two types of flower-forming classes are prerequisites to pruning and must be understood if pruning is attempted. The two classes are described as follows:

[39]

I.   Flowers that develop on shoots of the current year's growth are characterized by the following types of development:

A. If the flower is borne in the early spring on the end of a short shoot that originally burst forth from a winter bud, it is described as CO-TERMINAL, since the shoot at first elongates and bears leaves and axillary buds. The terminal end of the shoot finally forms a flower bud, which thus ends the axial growth of the shoot for the season. Thus, the description of the type can be understood readily because, with the formation of the flower, the growth of the shoot ends or terminates. This type of fruit-bud formation is found in the Quince, Hickory, Walnut, Medlar, and in some species of Maple. It is quite a common type found in nature among flowering plants.

B. When winter buds of the previous year's growth burst open and develop into a leafy shoot that finally terminates into a cluster of flower buds, this type is described as TERMINAL fruit-bud-formation, as illustrated in the panicles of the Raspberry, Blackberry, Dewberry, Loganberry, and the Orange. It is typical in our common garden roses.

C. If the shoot, originating as described under B, develops its fruit buds in the axil of the leaves, while the terminal growing point or bud continues elongating into a vegetative shoot, this type is described as LATERAL fruit formation. This is the type found in the Grape, Chestnut, Persimmon, Mulberry, and the Olive.

D. The final type of this first group is demonstrated

[40]

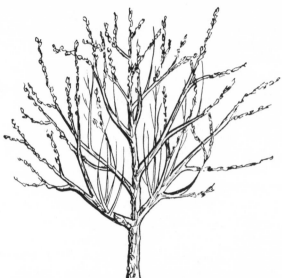

Apple—Before and After Pruning

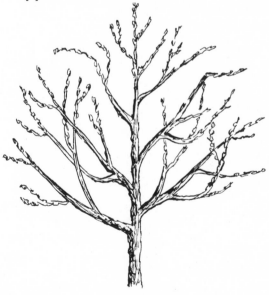

by the Loquat, in which the flower buds are developed terminally on terminal shoots.

II. The second class of fruit-bud production includes those plants in which the flowers are generally produced directly from existing winter buds. These are divided into 2 distinct forms:

A. In the first group the fruit buds are normally lateral and usually not borne on spurs. These include the Peach, Almond in most varieties, Apricot in some varieties, the Filbert, and the Hazelnut.

B. In the second group the buds in most of the varieties are developed on spurs or short stub branches, or in some species they are borne terminally. This type is illustrated in the Apple, Pear, Cherry, Plum in most varieties, Apricot in most varieties, Almond in some varieties, Currants in a few varieties, and the Gooseberry.

The following list of fruit plants includes suggestions on pruning with additional hints of specific care. A complete list of all the varieties known today would be impossible in this booklet. We suggest that you know your variety and study its behavior as to fruit-bud formation and how best to prune the variety after all of its specific habits of growth have been learned. Use sharp tools, good common sense, and take nothing for granted; a recorded behavior of a given variety within a specific district may not become the same record of the plant in your particular orchard.

ALMOND   *Prunus communis*

This nut tree is probably native to Western Asia and has been in cultivation since very ancient times. At present there are over 118 named varieties recognized. The almond nut is divided into 2 general tribes, the one representing the bitter-

[42]

tasting group which is used in the manufacture of flavoring extracts and prussic acid; the other group comprises the sweet, edible almonds. Frost is one of the major factors in failure of Almond production, since the trees bloom earlier than any of the other deciduous fruit-bearing trees. The second factor for failure is the sterility of many varieties, if they fail to have proper cross-pollination. They are fast-growing, robust, erect trees.

General pruning should be done in the dormant season. It should be limited to some thinning out, the removal of dead wood and cutting out crowding and rubbing branches. The flower buds form on one year old wood, or growth of the previous summer as described under class II, type A. Technical pruning is limited to cutting out the twigs that produced fruit the previous season and leaving one or two vegetative shoots that developed at the base from lateral buds of the fruiting shoot. These selected shoots will be the best fruit-producing shoots the next season. The resulting pruning is a topping operation, in a sense, in which the top is cut back to selected basal growth for the next year. If these remaining selected fruit branches are still too thick and crowding, thinning out is advisable. The height of the tree is no serious handicap in harvesting, since shaking the fruit down is not injurious to the fruit.

APPLE   *Pyrus malus*

The Apple, as we know it today, is thought to be native from southwestern Asia to the Mediterranean region of Europe. Its cultivation is older than recorded history of man, since charred fruit and seeds of the fruit have been found in the remains of prehistoric Lake Dwellers in Switzerland. Over 22 varieties were known to the Romans, and since that time hybridization has accounted for over 6500 horticultural forms; at present 418 varieties are recognized as standard.

The flowers are commonly borne on spurs as listed under class II B. The fruit-bud is recognized by the following characters: it is much larger than the wood-bud; it is usually very pubescent or hairy; it is wider than long; and it is much wider than the diameter of the spur that bears it. The fruit-bud does not increase the length of the spur once it is formed, but below it a vegetative bud may develop that is held in check or in a dormant condition while the fruit is maturing and absorbing all the nourishment sent into the spur branch. Once the fruit matures and is removed, the vegetative shoot gains its chance to grow out slightly during the next season and then it forms a fruit-bud for the following season. This accounts for the alternating fruit bearing seasons, particularly with most varieties of apples. There are some varieties that tend to bear fruit every year and can be induced to do so by June pruning and thinning out. The formation of fruit-buds is also related to a nutritional factor and seasonal pruning. We find that summer pruning is a stimulus to fruit-bud formation, while any other seasonal pruning is more conducive to vegetative or wood formation, particularly if the pruning is done in excess.

Pruning Apple trees has been basically discussed under our heading "Pruning fruit-bearing trees, shrubs, and vines." The narrow crotch, spaced lateral branches, and the pyramidal-shaped tree with a central axis are factors in the care of Apple trees. Thinning out is also essential to allow a little sunlight throughout the inner part of the tree. But do not clean out the inner part of the tree so that the limbs are stripped to nearly the end, suggesting a "Mule-tail." The maximum height of a tree depends on conditions and

[44]

varieties, but the average height should not exceed the need of using a ladder longer than 20 to 22 feet to pick the fruit from the top. Pruning in most orchards is done in the dormant season, at which time the heavy summer growth is thinned out and the general framework of the tree is retained, leaving the branches as evenly spaced as possible.

The process of topping lightly means the removal of 30% of the season's summer growth; it is thought to induce greater possible fruit-bud production. Heavy pruning means the removal of 60% of the season's new growth and results in a stimulus to vegetative or wood growth. The latter

Pruning thin wood growth allows sunlight to reach the inner part of an apple tree.

[45]

method is best for young trees that are making a normal, rapid growth. However, additional thinning of the fruit crop in June is wise, since the period between May to July is always characterized by the expression "June drop," which means that during this period a natural adjustment takes place between the amount of fruit that is on a branch and the amount that the limb can actually carry on to maturity. Some of the immature fruit will fall off.

One recent method of pruning suggests the removal of "thin wood." These are branches that are thin and tend to grow downward, particularly when laden with some fruit. The fruit produced on them is smaller and of poorer quality. These branches are usually crowded, shaded, and generally condemned as unproductive. Removal of "thin wood" is recommended in the spring months before the growth starts, or even better in June or July when the fruit is on the tree; pruning at this later period also thins out excess fruit.

APRICOT   *Prunus armeniaca*

The common Apricot of Europe and America is native to Asia where it still may be found in the wild. Records reveal that it has been in cultivation in China for 4000 years; it was undoubtedly introduced into Europe in the First century. In spite of its ancient cultivation, only 42 recognized orchard varieties are listed.

Pruning of the Apricot is quite similar to that of the Plum. The fruit-buds are borne on spurs, as the Apple, or on the wood of the previous season's growth, either terminal or lateral. Thus, the Apricot is listed under class II A and B. Before pruning a variety learn the habit of fruit-bud formation. If the variety is unknown to you, then study new growth and observe where the flowers develop. The fruit-bud is easily recognized; it is much larger in size than the wood-bud. In most varieties of Apricot the long slender shoots that grow during the summer months will bear the fruit the following season, but the location of the fruit-bud on the slender shoot is characteristic of the variety. There are 3 possible locations:

a. Towards the tip of the previous year's growth.

b. In the central part of the shoot.

c. Near the base of the shoot.

In any case, the fat buds produce the fruit, while the slender buds will open into leaves and branch growth. In pruning, do not cut back the tips if the variety is of class "a." In class "b," prune back about ⅓ of the shoot, and in class "c" top back ½ to ⅔ of the shoot. Of course general pruning is given the tree, cutting out enough branches to shape the top. A few varieties of Apricots also develop fruit on spurs formed on older wood. Do not remove these unless injured or for some other good reason, since their fruit is always strong, well-supported, and of good quality.

AVOCADO   *Persea americana*

This fruiting plant is native to Mexico, Central America, and in South America to Peru and Brazil. The name "Avocado" is an English corruption of the Spanish name "Ahuacate" or "Aquacate" which is based on the Aztec name "Ahuacatl." There are now over 433 forms recognized in the fruit industry.

Pruning is almost nil with this tropical species. Remove branches that die back immediately. Thinning out is dangerous, since the inside of the tree is sensitive to sunlight, which hardens the naturally green bark and slows down the flow of sap. Weak branches tend to droop when loaded with heavy leaves and fruit. When this happens with the outer,

[47]

lower branches, they gradually bend lower, year after year. These should be removed gradually, but do not make an opening or "hole" in the side of the tree permitting sunlight to penetrate the center. Also, one-sided trees can sometimes be corrected by clipping back gradually the heavy growth side; the sparse side will gain the extra food and fill out.

BLACKBERRY   *Rubus species*

The cultivated Blackberries are the domestication of several species of the genus Rubus. Most of the garden varieties originate from American species, but a few of recent introduction are from the Himalayan region. Over 63 varieties are listed as standard forms.

The general objective in pruning fruit-bearing bushes of which the Blackberry is a representative is to:

a. Increase the vigor of the plant.

b. Prolong the life of the bush by preventing over-bearing.

c. Increase the yield of the fruit by inducing larger and better fruit.

d. Keep the bramble within bounds for control, cultivation, and care.

The Blackberry is classed as a bramble or a fruit-bearing shrub that produces its fruit on canes one year old, as listed under class I B. First year planting requires no pruning; the plants may be permitted to sprawl at random. During the following winter the plants are either treated as a bush or tied to a trellis or frame. These first year old canes will bear fruit the following summer. New canes will also develop and these should be pinched at the terminal point when the canes are from 24 to 36 inches long, if the plants are to be bushes; if trained on a trellis, the canes may be permitted to grow up to 5 feet in length. During the dormant season the old canes that bore fruit are removed; many advise that these canes should be removed immediately after the fruiting period, since they may interfere with the growth of the new canes. The new canes that have been pinched back during the summer growth will develop long lateral branches, which should be cut back 8 to 12 inches. There is naturally an excess of canes; during the dormant season select from 4 to 7 of the best canes to a cluster or hill, or 2 to 3 per foot of a row; all other canes should be removed since there will be some winter injury in evidence and the excess canes will be of no value to the quantity and quality of the fruit.

BLUEBERRY   *Vaccinium species*

Fruit is obtained from approximately 20 species and varieties, long gathered wild in North America. New hybrid forms are now being developed and introduced, having better, larger, and sweeter fruit. The fruit is borne on wood of the previous season's growth, as listed under class II A. Pruning is usually light if at all; removal of dead wood, thinning out and cutting back, even removing some of the fruit aids in fruit production; otherwise the excess fruit will be very small. Pruning also induces new growth for the next season.

BUTTERNUT   *Juglans cinerea*

This American species has been improved and at present 23 cultural varieties are listed, based on the character of the nut. Since the fruit develops as listed under class I A, no formal pruning is required, other than the removal of injured, diseased, and faulty branches.

[49]

CASHEW   *Anacardium occidentale*

This valuable economic plant, native to tropical America, is most valued for its delicious nut. The grayish-brown coat or hull of the nut contains an oil suggestive of poison ivy, which irritates and blisters the skin of some people. Special pruning is not required.

CHERRY   *Prunus species*

The Sweet and Sour Cherry groups are varieties and hybrids of 2 species of *Eurasia*. These have been domesticated from the wild almost since prehistoric times. The Sour Cherry, *Prunus Cerasus,* is listed with over 300 varieties and forms, and at present 19 standard forms are recorded for the orchard. The Sweet Cherry, *Prunus Avium,* is credited with over 600 varieties of which 39 are standard in the orchard. The Duke type of Cherry, a hybrid between the 2 species of Sweet and Sour Cherries, is intermediate between the growth habit and fruit quality of the parents. Over 11 listed forms are recorded of this hybrid. Cherry flowers are borne on spurs; thus Cherries belong to class II B.

Pruning of the Cherries is confined to the early life of the trees; if well done, later yearly pruning is limited merely to removing poor wood and thinning. Since the fruit is not as heavy as that of apples or peaches, the pyramidal type of tree is not essential; in fact, many advise the open vase type of tree. Pruning, however, starts with the whip, the one year old planting, which has no secondary laterals, particularly in the Sweet Cherry group. The whip is clipped or topped back at planting time to about 24 to 36 inches from the ground, at least to the height of a low trunk, which is desirable. As laterals develop during the summer, select about 3 of these near the top and at least 6 to 8 inches apart if possible. Pinch out all the rest of the laterals. During

[50]

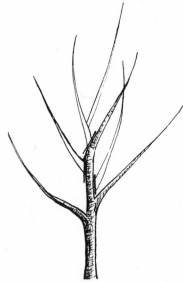

Shaping a Young Cherry Tree

the next dormant season top the framework or lateral branches that were permitted to grow to about ⅓ to ½ of their summer growth; during the following summer again select 2 shoots of each lateral that are well spaced on each of the 3 main laterals, and pinch out all the others that have developed. This is continued until the tree is 4 to 5 years old. By this method the erect habit of growth with poor, narrow crotch formation, characteristic of the Sweet Cherry, will be prevented and the tree will have the basis of an excellent framework. After this form is established, merely apply pruning principles for a healthy tree, removing interfering branches, injuries, and excess growth.

The Sour Cherry is not erect in habit. Thus, after 3 years of pruning, as suggested for the Sweet Cherry, it will need only thinning out the top or fruiting wood, to prevent its tendency to tangle up with small branch growth.

CURRANT   *Ribes species*

These berry bushes are derived mainly from European and American species of *Ribes* and at present over 59 forms are listed. Flowers of the red and white varieties are borne on 1 year old wood and on spurs which develop from wood 2 or more years old. Thus, currants are listed under class II A & B. The pruning is confined to removing canes after they have produced 3 successive crops of fruit. If a strong growth develops near the base of an old cane, cut to it; it may be considered as a new cane. Currants are natural bushes with many stems starting out both near and below the surface of the ground, and so more stems are formed than should be retained. Pruning consists of removing superfluous stems and canes that are more than 3 years old. The Black Currant group bears most of its fruit on wood of the previous season's growth, and consequently this group should be permitted to develop a supply of one year old healthy wood. Pruning is done in the dormant season.

DEWBERRY   *Rubus species*

The Dewberry is considered a trailing and climbing type of Blackberry. This fruit is of American origin and of recent domestication from wild species, of which over 30 varieties are now listed. Care of the bushes is similar to that of the Blackberry, excepting that they are trained on a trellis, never grown as a bush. Pruning consists of cutting back young canes to 4 or 5 feet in length the first year in which the plants are set out, to prevent too much sprawling; then cut out old canes after the fruiting period, and head in long shoots and laterals in early summer. Each plant is limited to from 4 to 6 canes.

FIG   *Ficus carica*

A native of Asia. Over 27 varieties are listed. If they are grown for table figs, they are headed low, usually about 18 to 24 inches from the ground. Trees grown for dried figs are permitted to have a longer trunk, so that the tree can be kept smooth and clean beneath, since the figs are usually allowed to ripen and fall and are gathered from the ground. A higher trunk makes this operation easier.

Fig varieties are listed in terms of color, as White, Brown, and Black. Since flower productions is of two distinct classes, pruning technique must be regulated accordingly. In the first system of pruning, which is applied to the White and Brown Fig varieties, the process is one of cutting back severely, since the flowers are borne on the season's new growth, as described under class I. The shoots that bore fruit the previous season are cut back to two eyes or bud scars. If the tree is in good health, each of the bud

Fig—Before and After Pruning

scars will send out a shoot in the spring growth upon which figs will be produced. These new shoots in the dormant period are again cut back; thus, pruning is carried on season after season. The framework of the tree should originally be started with a low head, about 24 inches from the ground and permitted to have no more than three lateral branches evenly spaced.

The second type of pruning is applied to the Black variety of figs. The fruit is borne on wood that is one year or more old. Start the tree with a low trunk, unless the tree is to be used also for shade, and permit the tree to develop three basic laterals the first year. After that, pruning consists only of thinning and removing poor branches and retaining a well balanced, evenly spaced top. Fig trees tend to "bleed" when cut; so prune only during the dormant period.

FILBERT   *Corylus species*

The Filbert of Europe is the Hazelnut of America. It is a type of nut obtained from species native to Europe. The species involved may be grouped or classified as follows:

a. True Filberts are obtained from *Corylus maxima;* the nut is provided with a tubular husk which is much longer than the nut itself, which is oblong in shape. The plant is tree-like in habit.

b. Cobs. The word cobs is applied to the nut of *Corylus Avellana,* the "European Hazelnut"; the husk is little or no longer than the nut, which is roundish and angular in shape. The plant is also tree-like in habit and is successfully cultivated in Oregon. This is the nut we refer to as Hazelnut in America. Over 231 varieties are listed, the forms being based on the character of the nut and the habit of the plant, which ranges from shrub-size to almost tree-

[55]

size. All of the species are monoecious in floral development; that is, male catkins and female flowers develop on different parts of the same plant, but from wood one year old. Pruning, hence, is limited to thinning out, removing injury, and a general shaping of the plant. Our true American Hazelnut develops small, roundish and thick-shelled nuts that can be eaten, but are usually not cultivated commercially.

GOOSEBERRY   *Grossulaira species*

Various wild species were probably first cultivated in Europe in the 16th century. Records show that the first American wild species of Gooseberry was domesticated in 1847. At present there are 45 listed forms. Pruning of the shrub is similar to the care of Currants, since they are closely related botanically. The shrub can almost take care of itself, but if size and quality of fruit are desired, pruning is advised. Since the fruit-bud develops on one year old wood, the bush does not bear fruit until the second year; thus the Gooseberry is listed under class II B. Usually pruning is not started until the bush is four years old, based on the fact that a branch after bearing three successive years will begin to decrease in its fruitful quality in the fourth fruiting year. The berries become smaller each following year. The old cane is thus cut out in the dormant season to new bearing wood, or in favor of younger shoots near the base. At least, cut back, leaving a stub from six to seven inches long from the ground; new shoots will sprout from this stub. This type of pruning will induce the formation of many shoots. In the spring allow only 3 or 4 of these shoots from the stub to grow; remove all the others. By careful selection there will be a continuous series of 1, 2, 3, and 4 year

[56]

Gooseberry—Before and After Pruning

wood present, resulting in a continuous fruit production. Suckers near the plants should be removed.

GRAPEFRUIT   *Citrus paradisi*

The Grapefruit or Pomelo undoubtedly originated some-where in Asia, either in China, Malaya, or Polynesia, as a sport of the Shaddock. The name "Grapefruit" originated from the West Indies as a descriptive native name applied to the fruit, which is often borne in clusters from 3 to 12 and more. The fruit-buds are borne terminal on the season's growth, as characteristic of all citrus fruit; the ends of the branches should not, in general, be pinched back. Thus, the tree is listed under class I B. When planted out, the young tree should be cut back, making a trunk from 18 to 24 inches high and so forming a low headed tree. After that, only injuries, bad limbs, and possible frost kill should be removed. The lower limbs should also be cut back so that they are high enough to keep them off the ground when they are loaded with fruit. If new growth is too vigorous in young trees, it is wise to check it and keep the general shape of the tree. Excess suckers may also be removed and some author-ities advise light thinning.

GRAPES   *Vitis species*

The Grape is one of the oldest of domesticated fruits of man; it probably originated in the Caspian Sea region of Western Asia. Grapes have been grown in Egypt for 6000 years, were highly developed by the Greeks and Romans, and were frequently mentioned in the Bible. The European Grape, known botanically as *Vitis vinifera* means "wine-bearing Vitis," and is the "Vine" of the ancients. At pres-ent there are over 408 varieties listed as standard.

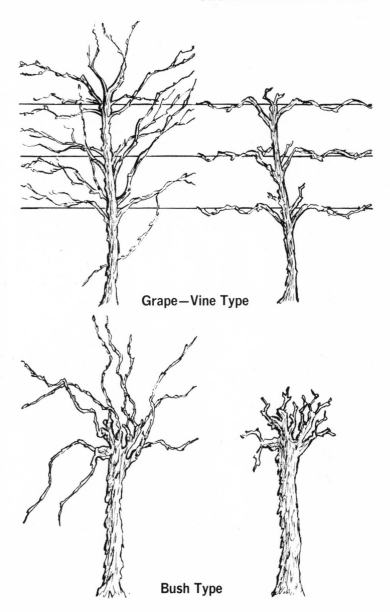

Grape—Vine Type

Bush Type

Pruning of the Grape is not a difficult process. By studying the flower-bud formation we learn that the Grape produces its fruit on wood of the current year, from winter buds on canes that developed the previous season; this type is under class I C. Grapes are divided into two cultural groups: the bush type, and the vine.

The specific pruning care of the bush type, which is applied mostly to the European species, *Vitis vinifera,* starts the second year after planting; the first year's care of the plant is limited to training the plant. Allow one strong, selected cane to grow, removing all lateral growth from it; all other canes should be cut out. This cane is staked and tied at intervals to keep it upright and straight, because it is to become the trunk of the bush, forming in a sense the beginning of a miniature tree. During the dormant season the cane is cut back to about 2 or 3 inches above the top of the stake, the height of the stake being determined by the grower (the average is 2 feet from the ground). In the spring allow only 2 top buds to send out shoots, cutting off all others and removing them smoothly so that no laterals may develop at the point of cutting. The 2 canes may be permitted to grow during the summer and establish the bush with a good root system. The following dormant season is the beginning of the annual pruning of the bush Grape. All canes that develop on the mature bush during the summer should be cut back to ½ to ¾ of an inch above the second eye, or bud, at the base of the cane. If one bud is injured or killed, another will always be present to carry on, and if the plant is vigorous, both buds may grow; do not remove the extra growth since both new canes will bear fruit the next season. The time of pruning is best during the dormant period, soon after the leaves have fallen; there is no danger of "bleeding" then. Many prefer pruning during a late

[60]

Early training of the central trunk is important for successful growth.

winter thaw, in February or early March, reasoning that then all "winterkill" can be detected and removed. The stake or brace originally used should be removed as soon as the trunk is strong enough to support its crown. The trunk can become extremely aged, as attested to in old vineyards of the Old World.

When training a bush type of Grape on an arbor or trellis one must observe the early training of the central trunk; this is started with a main, long cane trained vertically up the side of the arbor. When the cane has reached the top of the arbor, permit a central crown of a series of lateral canes to develop. These may be trained to grow either fan-wise or radially from the trunk to be, or they may be arranged in parallel rows on top of the arbor, if we space them 12 to 15 inches apart. These horizontal permanent canes are allowed to grow sufficiently long to become the foundation for a series of crowns at their ends from which new canes will develop to be the source of the fruit. The ends of the permanent canes will be the crowns treated by the 2 eye method, as described for the bush type.

The vine-type of pruning is applied specifically to American species of Grapes, which are natural climbers and do best when permitted to grow on a trellis. Many systems are used in America, based on the 3-wired fence type of trellis. Basically, a trunk is started similar to the bush type, but once established, pruning is not limited to 2 eyes but to 3 to 5 eyes, resulting in a cane about 3 to 4 feet long. Select 6 of the best canes, training 3 canes in one direction and 3 in the opposite, removing all others. Canes ¼ of an inch thick are the best to select; thicker ones show vigorous growth, but they are called "Bull Canes" and, in general, bear inferior bunches of grapes. This type of pruning permits the development of from 30 to 75 bunches of Grapes to a plant, thus giving bigger clusters, larger Grapes, greater weight, and the fruit with a better flavor. The harvest rewards this method remarkably in spite of the severe pruning. The arbor method of treating the vine-type is similar to the bush-type, excepting that the fruiting canes should be longer, with 3 to 5 eyes.

A grape vine trimmed to three canes on either side of the trunk permits development of bigger clusters, larger grapes and better flavor.

[63]

HAZELNUT   *See Filbert*

HICKORY   *Carya species*

The nut of several species of *Carya*. The Hickory species
bear co-terminal flowers, as described under class I A; thus
no specific pruning is required. The outstanding Hickory
is the Pecan, Carya pecan, of which over 110 varieties are
now listed. The Pecan is strictly of American origin. Paper-
shelled varieties are now available and they can be broken
open with the fingers. Pecan trees are usually started as
seedlings and then top-grafted; when once established, and
the tree bears properly with a good quality of nut, it needs
only general pruning. The common Shagbark Hickory,
Carya ovata, is listed with 17 varieties. The nuts of all other
species of Hickory are usually too bitter to cultivate; nuts
are gathered only from natural, wild plants.

HUCKLEBERRY   *Gaylussacia species*

This is an American berry, mostly collected from wild
bushes, particularly from the species *Gaylussacia baccata.*
The Blueberries, which are closely related, are more popular, but the Huckleberry may some day be cultivated and
improved. Pruning would be similar to that of the Blueberry.

LEMON   *Citrus limonia*

The Lemon has been in cultivation in the Old World for
over 2000 years. It is a native of southeastern Asia. It must
have reached India at a very early date, for there is a San-
skrit word for the fruit. The flower-bud develops terminally
on shoots of the current year, as described under class I B.
Pruning, primarily, is keeping the trees low and compact.
The trees tend to produce long, bare branches tufted with
leaves at the terminal ends and without fruiting twigs; these

[64]

should be headed in to cause the development of fruit, well in toward the center of the trees. Some advise that no special pruning is required the first 4 years after the young trees are set out, except to remove rubbing branchlets, particularly those that develop on the trunk of the tree. Rub off or pull these out instead of cutting; otherwise the wound may induce the formation of adventitious buds. The tendency to shoot out long, upright shoots, as described above, is a natural habit; most of these shoots will gradually bend down and become the basis of a good fruit-bearing foundation. Some advise to retain these and not head them in, claiming that these shoots should become the cyclic fruit-bearing foundation of the tree. The method is as follows: the shoots that develop in the center of the tree during the summer months will in time produce fruit; select only one or two of the best and remove the rest. This shoot will form lateral branches as it reaches the top of the tree, and the heavy weight of the leaves and fruit will bend it down. By this constant yearly selection of inner central shoots which bend over, there will be a series of fruiting branches of diverse ages. The oldest shoot will finally bend too far, and when it is within 2 feet from the ground, it must be removed. The age of this type of fruiting limb, from the sucker year to the time it must be removed, is from 5 to 10 years. The above system may be continued yearly, thus constantly renewing fruit-bearing wood. The tree, however, under this type of treatment is not very symmetrical, but it does produce fruit.

LIME   *Citrus aurantifolia*

The Lime was orginally domesticated from wild plants of southeastern Asia. It is a tropical tree and very sensitive to cold temperature. There are about 11 varieties listed. Usually they are grown from seedlings, and the fruit is named according to the districts from which it originates, as "Key," "West Indian," or "Mexican Lime." There is no specific pruning required other than thinning out and making the inner part of the tree accessible, since the branches are very sharp-thorny.

LOQUAT   *Eriobotrya japonica*

The Loquat, known also as "Biwa," is native to China and Japan. It has long been cultivated in these countries. There are now 12 varieties for the orchard. The flower-bud formation is quite distinct, as listed under class I D. Special pruning is not required other than to thin out some of the branches at intervals in order to permit some light to enter into the center of the tree. Naturally, dead wood should be removed, and suckers that develop inside the tree should also be pulled off; suckers that develop from the roots close to the surface must be discouraged. Prune early in fall.

MANGO   *Mangifera indica*

This is one of the oldest of important tropical fruits. It has been in cultivation for over 6000 years. It is a native of southern Asia. It is cultivated now in Malaya, Polynesia, Africa, tropical America, and in southern Florida and California. Over 500 horticultural varieties are now listed. Special pruning is not required other than the general care given to tropical trees.

MEDLAR   *Mespilus germanica*

The plant is a close relative of the Apple, and is native to Europe and Asia Minor. Several varieties are cultivated, particularly in England. The brown, Apple-shaped fruit has a harsh flesh and is of rather acid taste. There is no special pruning required other than that applied to the Apple.

[66]

NECTARINE   *Prunus persica, var. nectarina*

The Nectarine is literally a smooth-skinned Peach. It was once thought to be a species; others have considered it as a variety of the Peach, as named above. To-day it is definitely thought of as a hybrid, often arising from seeds of Peaches and also from seeds of its own fruit. Once a hybrid is established and proven of merit, it becomes a selected variety for grafting. Over 60 hybrids of this type are now listed. Pruning is very similar to that of the Peach, excepting that it is not necessary to prune as severely. See suggestions for pruning the Peach tree.

OLIVE   *Olea europeae*

This tree has been domesticated since prehistoric times. It was well known in Egypt 3700 years ago and is frequently mentioned in the Bible and in Greek and Roman literature. The species is still found wild from the Punjab, India, to Morocco and the Canary Islands.

The Olive tree is grown both as an ornamental and for fruit. It can stand most severe pruning and shaping, but usually it is not pruned when grown as an ornamental. Its gnarled habit of growth makes the tree seem most exotic in appearance. When cultured for fruit, it needs pruning to prevent the gnarled habit. The tree is topped, and ill-placed branches are removed during the first and second year of its planting. After the second year the lower branches should be removed to form a clean trunk 2 to 3 feet high. If the tree becomes close and compact in growth, thinning out the excess branches is wise. A good scaffold should be formed by the time the tree is 5 to 6 years old. The annual pruning of the mature tree involves thinning out ⅓ to ½ of the small branches, especially those that bore fruit the previous year. The fruit develops laterally on current year's growth, as de-

[67]

scribed under Class I C. If pruning is neglected, the fruit becomes smaller each season.

ORANGE   *Citrus sinensis*

The *Sweet Orange* or *Common Orange*, is native to southeastern Asia, either from China or Indo-China. Records reveal the Orange was cultivated 1500-1000 B. C. It was introduced very early in India, and into Europe in the 14th century. The Spaniards were responsible for its introduction into America. Other important species also cultivated are the "Sour Orange," or "Seville Orange," *Citrus aurantium;* the "King Orange," *Citrus nobilis,* which includes varieties comprising the group known as "Mandarins," "Tangerines," and the "Satsuma Orange"; "Citron," *Citrus medica;* and the "Calamondin" or "Panamo Orange," *Citrus mitis*. At present there are 107 Orange types listed in the grove markets.

The flower-buds form terminally on the current year's growth, as listed under class I B. Very little pruning is necessary, once the trees are established, other than shaping up the trees and removing dead and injured wood or diseased branches. Most of the pruning is done when the tree is young, to give it a good symmetrical and spreading form with a short trunk. This type of shape permits good shade for the center and trunk of the tree. Too much thinning is not advisable, but the control of excess suckers if they form within the tree is necessary.

PEACH   *Prunus persica*

The Peach is a native of China where it has been in cultivation for thousands of years. Many varieties were developed in ancient times by the Chinese, and the fruit has had many legends associated with it. The fruit was introduced

[68]

into the Mediterranean region in early times, since the Romans knew at least 6 varieties. At present, there are 337 standard varieties listed for the orchard. The flower-buds burst out from existing winter buds of the previous year's new growth, as listed under class II A.

The trunk of the tree should be about 18 to 24 inches high; some allow the trunk to be 4 feet high. The lateral branches should be at least 8 inches apart and at good angles, not too narrow. The tree is comparatively shortlived; as soon as the tree fails to respond to pruning and produces poor fruit, the tree should be removed.

The aim of the pruner is to secure young growth fairly distributed over all parts of the tree, so selected that all

Peach trees benefit more from heavy pruning, bearing greater quality as well as quantity of fruit.

[69]

parts are in full exposure to light. An unpruned Peach tree will in a few years have comparatively slender branches almost without foliage, and the little fruit that is produced will be formed only at the extreme ends of the branches. The entire length of the previous year's growth will burst into flowers, but the best section of the flowering branch is the central ⅓ of the shoot; thus, the pruner definitely aims to cut back ⅓ of all new growth. The method of procedure of pruning the Peach tree is:

a. Cut out all dead branches; the older the tree, the greater number of these branches will be present. If the tree is more than 10 years old, it is wise to select new branches from the central framework of the tree to replace old limbs which have become diseased, broken, or too old.

b. Remove wood that produced fruit last year; it will not produce again; also cut out crossing or rubbing branches, and branches that do not contribute to the general form of the tree.

c. The shape of the tree should be funnel-like, the center being open, permitting sunlight to penetrate all parts of the tree. This aids in ripening the fruit.

d. Thin out branches throughout the tree to even its balance, always favor new growth, but if a vigorous branch has exceeded the contour of the tree, cut it back; these elongated branches may snap when loaded with fruit; Peach wood is very brittle.

e. Cut back the ⅓ of new growth, always bearing in mind that fruiting branches should be about 1 foot apart over the top of the tree.

When the task is done properly, the pruner should have at least 65% of the tree on the ground. This is severe pruning, but the Peach tree benefits more by heavy pruning of this nature than any other fruit tree. Even the removal of

[70]

Peach—Before and After Pruning

old wood is a form of rejuvenation of the tree. Often one is forced to cut out as much as 70 to 75% of the previous year's growth, but it benefits fruit production in quality and size. A healthy tree will set a large amount of fruit after pruning. During early June the tree will drop a portion of its unripe fruit as a reduction process. Thinning out additional fruit is advised after the "June drop," as suggested under Apples. A little summer pruning is also advisable. Varieties that make a late growth may be caught by a frost while their leaves are still immature and the terminal tips of the shoots are still succulent or juicy; these should be cut back at once, removing all of the immature areas injured, cutting back even to 2 to 3 year old wood. By this precaution it may save the tree from becoming badly affected with disease, which often follows the freezing of unripe wood. If this happens, all other pruning should be delayed for a year, so the tree may recover. Heavy pruning of winter or frost injured trees frequently causes the death of the tree.

PEAR   *Pyrus species*

The Pears are obtained primarily from 3 botanical groups of species:

1. The European Pear, *Pyrus communis,* which comprises most of the old, standard varieties.

2. The Oriental or Asian Pear, *Pyrus pyrifolia;* this species is native to China, the fruit is very gritty, hard-fleshed, but of a long keeping quality.

3. The Eurasian Hybrid. A hybrid between the above 2 species, the Kieffer and Leconte being typical hybrids of this group.

The Pear has been known since ancient times, and at present there are 112 standard forms of Pears listed for the orchard. The varieties are most diversified in their habit of growth, being either dwarf or tall trees. Pruning, however, is applied similarly to all varieties, and in general they are treated and trained as stated for the Apple tree. The flowers are definitely borne on spurs, as listed under class II B. Pruning favors spur-production, but at no time should there be an excess in pruning. The Pear tree is much more erect in habit than the Apple tree and often develops very narrow crotches; these are not as serious with the Pear as with the Apple, since the tree can more readily survive a break at this point.

The pruner should aim to develop a semi-pyramidal type of tree, with a good framework of subordinate, lateral branches. Cutting back ⅓ of the elongated new growth favors the spur-formation at the base of each new shoot cut. The middle ⅓ of the shoot produces the best fruit. Also remove or thin out excess new growth, particularly near the center of the tree. Thinning out the top of the tree permits sunlight to penetrate throughout the tree; this exposure of the heart of the tree is essential to ripening of the fruit. Light summer pruning tends to check wood-growth and also favors the spurs. These spurs bear each year, unless injured by wind-whipped branches, disease, a careless climber, badly placed ladders, or by old age. Thinning excess fruit is done simply by removing some of the fruit spurs. The annual pruning of an established tree is limited to the removal of crowding and crossing branches. Sucker growth is ever present, particularly within the center of the tree; this should always be kept in check or it will soon crowd the heart of the tree by either forcing the tree into height or subjecting the tree to the dread disease known as "Pear or Fire Blight." This is a bacterial disease and spreads readily when branches are too close together, as in the case of excess, central sucker growth. The "Blight" spreads by spores, often

[73]

Pear Blossoms

entering the flower blossoms nearest the outer part of the tree, or through open wounds of cut branchlets. When the disease is active it spreads downward toward the heart of the tree, killing first the leaves, then the twigs, branchlets and the limbs. It must be removed immediately by cutting well beyond the visible infection from 6 to 8 inches. It can be easily recognized by the dull, coppery appearance of the underside of the dead branches or limbs. Always clean the cutting tools; they may be coated with spores, and be sure to burn up the branches with the disease. This disease is one of the main reasons why Pear trees should not be trimmed too severely, for wounds invite the spores.

PECAN   *See Hickory* under *Carya pecan*

PERSIMMON   *Diospyros species*

Our American species, *Diospyros virginiana,* has some noteworthy varieties now available. The small fruit of our speices, however, has never been too popular in America. The species is much used as stock for grafting on it the oriental types. The Persimmon most common in the market is primarily a strain of the oriental species, *Diospyros kaki,* introduced from China and Japan where over 800 varieties are grown. It is commonly known as "Oriental or Japanese Persimmon" or "Kaki". There are now 43 standard varieties listed.

Pruning of the Persimmon, in general, is not required once the tree is established, other than to keep the tree in good shape by general, light thinning and keeping the fruit-bearing branches well spaced. Some top the trees when they have become too tall and the fruit is difficult to pick. Many new branches will spring up from the headed or topped tree; these should be thinned out and the best retained. The young tree, however, must be treated specifically, training

[75]

for a strong crotch and well spaced lateral branches, since the Persimmon wood is rather brittle and snaps off readily. The flowers are borne dominantly on current season's growth, and the tree is of class I C.; occasionally fruit is also developed on 1 year old wood. One must also remember that the genus *Diospyros* is dioecious in flower development. This means that individual trees bear only male or female flowers. Hybrids may be exceptional. Be certain to check this; otherwise both male and female trees must be present to assure the formation of fruit.

PLUM   *Prunus species*

There are three main sources of the Plum that are used in our orchards today. These groups are all species of the genus *Prunus* and are listed as follows:

1. European species. The species of greatest antiquity and associated with history is *Prunus domestica,* undoubtedly originating in southeastern Asia where it may still be found growing wild. This species has been in cultivation for over 2000 years and was known, through records, to the Lake Dwellers, the Greeks, and the Romans. Over 900 varieties have been cultivated, particularly in Europe. This species includes the popular varieties "Green Gages," "Egg Plums," and many of the "Prunes." *Prunus insitita* has also been grown for over 2000 years and is still found wild in Europe and Asia; this species, which some botanists consider only as a variety of *Prunus domestica,* includes the "Damson" and "Bullace Plums." The "Sloe," *Prunus spinosa,* also called the "Blackthorn," is much used in Europe in making liquor.

2. American species. Many American species have been domesticated in recent times, chiefly *Prunus americana* of which some 260 forms have been developed, such as

[76]

"Blackhawk," "Hawkeye," and "De Sota." *Prunus hortu-lana* was the parent of "Cumberland," "Golden Beauty," and "Wayland." *Prunus nigra* was the source of "Cheney," "Itaska," and many others; these varieties of the last species are used mostly for preserves and marmalades.

3. Japanese species. *Prunus salicina* is the most important of the oriental species of which nearly 100 new varieties and hybrids have been developed, particularly by Burbank.

In general, the present list of standard forms now recorded of all types of Plums totals 354. The flowers of most varieties are borne on spurs, as described under class II B. The pruning of the Plums and Prunes is thus performed to favor spur production. The training is essentially the same as that suggested for Apple trees, except that the trees should be trained to a vase or funnel shape, not with a semi-pyramidal or central axis. This type of shape will result in having the center of the tree well covered with stubby spur-development which will produce fruit year after year. After the young trees have been cut to form a short trunk from 18 to 24 inches with a scaffold of 3 to 5 laterals with good crotch angles, very little pruning should be done other than the removal of dead, rubbing, and crossing branches, until the tree begins to bear fruit. Wood growth is much less in mature trees. Pruning then consists of keeping the vase shape of the tree, removing dead or damaged branches, shortening or cutting back the current season's growth to keep the young twigs in a vigorous growing condition and to thinning out spurs to prevent overbearing. If the trees are becoming taller than desired, there is no harm in heading back, usually cutting back to vigorous side branches. In the Japanese varieties, pruning is similar to that advised for the Peach tree, but it must not be as severe. Pruning is done

[77]

during the dormant period, preferably in late winter or early spring. Many advise allowing the long slender branches of some varieties to grow, permitting them to remain until they have produced a crop, which they will do in the second season. When these slender whips bend too low and possibly interfere with the tree, they are cut back to the crown from which they are replaced by new slender shoots.

Some advise clipping the new growth of the top of the tree ⅔ to ¾ of its length, until the tree is about 10 years old and has the desired form. New branches, they suggest, should be removed entirely if they are of no benefit to the form of the tree. The ideal shape is to have the branches about 1 foot from each other, thus making for easier picking and permitting light to penetrate. When the trees are 10 years old, it is suggested by many to cut out all new growth, leaving only replacement of branches for limbs that had to be removed, and keeping the balance of the tree. Since the spurs are in the center of the tree, they should be well protected; it is best to harvest the fruit from a ladder instead of standing on limbs within the tree.

POMEGRANATE   *Punica granatum*

This species is native to Iran. It has been in cultivation for centuries and reached the Mediterranean region and southern Asia in early times. The tree was grown in the famous Hanging Gardens of Babylon. The Pomegranate, which in natural growth habit is a shrub, may be trained into a tree from 15 to 20 feet high. There are now 11 varieties listed for the orchard.

Pruning of the plant is very simple. A great many shoots spring from the base of the plant, a natural shrub habit of the species; these must always be pruned, since they draw out the food from the fruit-bearing stems within the tree. The tree must be controlled by severe pruning of laterals, pulling them out as they appear. The flower buds are borne from any wood after it is 1 year old. If the tree is well topped, thinned and opened, it will produce excellent fruit, since the central part of the tree needs plenty of sunlight. Pruning is done during the dormant season.

PRUNE   *Prunus domestica*

Prunes are Plums with a high sugar content. The European species, *Prunus domestica,* is the source of all the Prune varieties. Pruning is similar to that given under the Plum.

QUINCE   *Cydonia oblonga*

The Quince has been cultivated since ancient times, having been highly esteemed by the Romans. The species is native to western Asia from Iran to Turkestan. It is still found as a wild plant. In spite of its intensive cultivation the plant has retained much of its wild character, though there are 12 horticultural forms listed. The flower-bud is formed co-terminally on the current season's wood, as listed in class I A. This type of flowering requires very little special pruning. However, the nature of the shrub does necessitate some careful pruning attention; otherwise the bush or tree will become too thick and densely compact, losing its shape and making it difficult to harvest the fruit. To set out young plants, trim young trees to a short whip. Keep the trunk short and train an open and well-spread tree. One must not forget the floral habits of the plant. Since the flowers arise from the ends of the current growth, clipping back the tree ends would remove all of the winter buds that should produce fruiting shoots. The best fruit is borne from current wood of lateral buds in the upper half of 1 year old twigs. These same branches will produce good new wood for 3 to 4 years;

Dead or broken canes should be pruned from row plantings of raspberries during the dormant season.

thin these out after that age. This is the only special pruning required besides a little thinning out. Some prefer a bush plant to the tree, however, the bush type being easier to train.

RASPBERRY   *Rubus species*

The Raspberries are varieties of various species of *Rubus*. The first forms introduced into America were types of European origin of the species, *Rubus idaeus*. The European Raspberry has been cultivated since ancient times, and was highly esteemed by the Greeks and the Romans. These are of the red-berry group. The "Common or American Red Raspberry" is obtained from the native species, *Rubus idaeus var. strigosus* (the *Rubus strigosus* of some botanists). The "Black Raspberry," *Rubus occidentalis,* is also of American origin.

Pruning is very simple and in many respects similar to that of the Blackberries and other bramblers. The flowers are borne on wood or canes developed the previous season, as described under class I B. Over 93 varieties are now listed for the berry. There are 2 types of culture for Raspberries: the hill method, and the solid row system. In the hill culture the plants are set out 5 feet apart and tied to stakes. In the row type of culture the plants are set 3 to 4 feet apart and trained on a trellis. In the red varieties the canes are not pinched back during their summer growth, such pruning inducing weaker shoots to form from the ground, instead of forcing out laterals. In the dormant season, cut out all broken or badly diseased canes; eliminate the ones outside the row if trained in this manner and cut the canes back to 3 feet, unless they are to be trained to a stake or under the hill method. In hill culture do not leave too many canes, the average being 4 to 6 canes per hill.

[81]

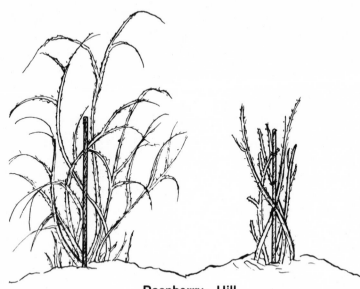

Raspberry—Hill

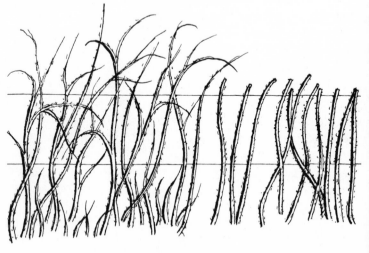

Raspberry—Row

The Black Raspberry types are treated differently. In this group the new canes, developing during summer growth, are pinched back to 24 inches in height or higher, if they are to be tied to stakes or on a trellis. This pinching back induces lateral branches to form. In the dormant season or early spring all the old dead fruiting canes are cut to the ground, if they were not removed after the fruit was harvested. All new canes not pinched back the previous season should be cut to the desired height if they are needed; otherwise remove entirely as too excessive. Finally cut back the laterals that formed during the previous season on the pinched canes to a length of 4 to 6 inches; longer laterals will produce more berries but they will be much smaller. Some advise longer laterals than the length suggested above, but we find this length the best. Others suggest that all fruiting canes of Raspberries should be removed immediately after the harvest of the fruit is completed, claiming that the new root shoots or canes will have a better chance to develop without too much interference.

WALNUT   *Juglans species*

There are three major groups of Walnuts of economic importance. These are:

1. The English Walnut, *Juglans regia.* The word "Walnut" is of Anglo-Saxon derivation, signifying "Foreignnut," which it really is in spite of its common name, since the English Walnut is native to Iran. It has been in cultivation for many centuries and at present there are 126 varieties listed.

2. Black Walnut, *Juglans nigra.* This is one of the important and valuable timber trees of our deciduous forests in the eastern United States. The nuts are most characteristic in flavor, and though they can be eaten raw, the

chief market for them is in the candy and ice-cream industry. The timber of the tree is, however, of greater value than the nut, though there are over 69 types of Black Walnuts listed.

3. East Asian Walnut, *Juglans sieboldiana*. This nut is not so well-known in the United States.

All of the Walnut species bear their flower-buds co-terminally on the current year's growth, as listed under class I A; thus, special pruning is not required. Young trees of the English Walnut that are from 6 to 10 feet high when set out are cut back to 5 feet. Some growers are more severe, cutting the whip back to 18 inches and then training a

Farm manager John Keck chooses a frosty day to trim the tops and sides of his raspberries.

lateral to become the leader until it reaches a height of 5 feet. This severe heading back results in a more vigorous tree compared to those that were originally cut back to 5 feet. Some advise cutting the whip back to 8 feet allowing no laterals to form within the lower 6 feet of the shoot. A good framework of 3 to 4 branches, widely spaced, is recommended. After this initial pruning, no specific care is necessary other than to thin out the poor, weak, and crowding branches. Outer branches may hang low in time and interfere with cultivation; these should be cut off during the winter months and new shoots permitted to replace them. The Black Walnuts are treated similarly.

Tying the grapes with soft tape.

Chapter Five

FRUIT-BEARING TREES, SHRUBS AND VINES

PLANTS CULTIVATED for their fruit are always under a handicap; the impossible is expected of them. In nature, a wild fruit tree never over-bears to become a burden or a hazard. There is a balance between the amount of fruit developed and the mechanical structure of the plant to bear the load. But in an orchard the plant is often forced far beyond its mechanical capacity to hold the load of fruit it is expected to produce. If given time, a branch by the stimulus of strain does develop cells within its anatomical structure by the process of growth, cells developing where the most need for strength is required; but this takes a bit of time. A wild tree bears its fruit in proportion to the strength of its limbs that must support the crop. Over-loading and over-sized fruit conditions of the tree are rare problems in nature; if it happens, the plant simply loses its branches and may even die while less vigorous plants survive, a basic law

[87]

of the survival of the fittest in natural selection. The orchard tree, however, is expected often to produce twice its natural load of fruit, both in size and weight, to be even considered a good fruit-bearer; yet often no thought is given to the limb, as to whether it is twice as strong to bear the doubled load.

A pruner should always remember and bear in mind that he is expected to induce the maximum amount of fruit by pruning; he should also realize that there must be just as much thought given to the mechanical support of the tree that is expected to bear the fruit loads. He should consider the stress, the elasticity of the branches, their sway and bend during high winds and storms, and the excess weight of the fruit they must bear. He should always consider the strength of the weakest point of the limb. But where is the weakest point of a fruit-bearing branch? Is it at the end of the branch, the highest point of the arch when the branch is bent with the load, or is it at the crotch, the point of attachment to the trunk of the tree? A walk through an orchard after a severe storm reveals the point of breakage and answers the problem quickly.

The pruner will naturally follow the basic laws of pruning as applied to all classes of plants, whether the trees are grown as shade, timber, forest, ornamental or fruit trees and shrubs. Weak limbs, suckers, diseased conditions and injuries, all must be removed. The pruner knows that fruit-bearing plants are subject to injuries, over-crowding, crossing and rubbing of limbs, and that branches must be removed; there are no exceptions. Thus, if he walks through an orchard, he can at a glance recognize the condition of the plants, whether they have been neglected and for how long, whether they had originally been started with a good framework when the trees were but a year or two old, and

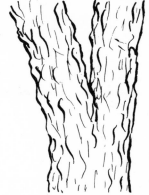

Weak Crotch—Too Narrow

Spacing of Branches

Middle Branch Crowded

Excellent Angle: 30-70

whether the basic structures of the trees are sufficiently strong and well placed, one limb in relation to the other. The most serious breaks to be observed will often be at the crotch of a tree, where the whole side of the tree may have split off or be hanging from the trunk of the tree. In this instance, the weakest point of the branch was at the crotch.

THE WEAK CROTCH OF A FRUIT TREE

The crotch of a fruit tree is at the point of attachment of a lateral branch to the main trunk or to the leader. Apparently the angle of the crotch determines its strength. Let us examine this more closely since it is most important, and if there is a "weak angle" let us investigate what could be done about it. A narrow crotch is most objectionable, since it proves to be very weak compared to a wider crotch. This type of crotch could be avoided in the early stages of growth of the tree by the process of selection. When the "whip" or single-stemmed plant is set out, no narrow-angled laterals should be selected. The following illustrations show the right and wrong angles of a crotch.

The figure marked A illustrates the narrow crotch, which is comparatively weak in many species of fruit trees, particularly in apple trees. It is always the first point to split off, if the limb is over-loaded and stressed with a high wind or storm of heavy rain or sleet. The ready cleavage of this type of crotch can be easily demonstrated. If a tree is cut down, note how much easier a narrow crotch is split with an axe than a crotch that is wide. The wood of the narrow crotch is apt to run with the grain, whereas the wood of a wider crotch would be arranged more against the grain and be stronger, as illustrated in figure C. True, the crotch does have a "heal" into the trunk, but it is proportionally narrow to the angle of the crotch. A right-angle and wider crotch is equally bad. The anatomy of a narrow crotch is provisionally strong enough to hold a normal weight, but excess weights are a handicap.

In the figure B we see 2 lateral branches almost opposite a central stem. This type of branching is very weak. Both laterals are weak since the crotches are too narrow, and if they do not split off during the life time of the tree, they will crowd out the central trunk and eventually kill it. If the central trunk is thus snuffed out, its stump is always a possible seat of decay. These conditions would never exist if the original plant had been properly pruned.

BRACING WEAK CROTCHES

If orchard trees have weak crotches due to early improper pruning, the trees should not be condemned and destroyed. If they are producing fruit, they should be preserved as well as possible. The weak crotch can be strengthened by means of braces, which should partly correct a bad situation. Bolts directly through the crotch are usually not enough to strengthen these weak cleavage points. The best method is by the use of screw eyes set high on the limbs involved, and if a third and a fourth limb can be included, it would assure even greater strength. If only 2 limbs are involved, a double, heavy wire is laced through the screw eyes and the wire is twisted taut by means of a pipe inserted through the middle of the wire strands. The pipe is turned, twisting the strands together. The wire should be heavy enough so that it will retain the twist. If more limbs are utilized, then the wires are laced from the screw eyes to a central loop of wire and pulled tight against the loop. Other methods of bracing may be used, but the main objective is to prevent the limb from hanging and straining at the narrow crotch. A water sprout or small lateral branchlet, if

[91]

available along the upper part of the limb, may be inarched across to another branch or to the trunk or leader, and induced to become a graft, serving as a brace.

A pruner may also relieve the crotch strain by pruning the limb rather severely and reducing some of the load of fruit and wood. There is a natural elasticity necessary for

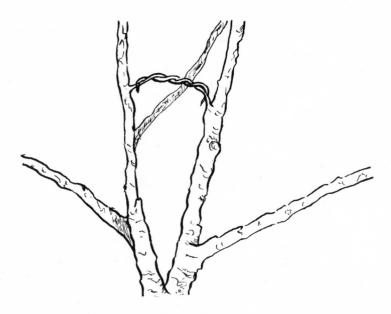

Natural brace

all limbs of a tree so that they may sway readily with sharp gusts of wind and "ride out" the blast as one would say. If they are too stiff, they may snap somewhere throughout their length.

SOME GENERAL HINTS

The horizontal crotch is often a source of future trouble. If possible, it should be removed when the tree is young. If one branch is directly above another, it is wise to remove the lower; the upper branch will eventually rub the lower and crowd it out. Often two or more branches may arise at the same point on a trunk; one must be selected, the other should be removed or dwarfed.

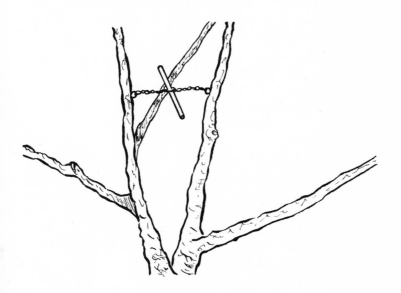

Wire brace

Excessive pruning of fruit trees is never advisable, since it may jeopardize the production of fruit. A little pruning is much better than none or too much.

Many fruiting plants are hybrids and do not respond to pruning in the same manner as natural species or varieties of nature. Their peculiarities should be learned. Usually they require excessive "pampering" not applicable to a

[93]

hardy Maple or a sturdy Oak. Their fruit buds may develop in most surprising ways, and these characters must be learned before specific pruning is practiced. Sometimes the growth of hybrids is most vigorous and excessive; on the other hand it may be suppressed or dwarfed, and if not watched properly, the stock upon which the hybrid is grafted may choke it out.

Training of a fruit tree during the first and second year after planting is the most critical period. This is the time when a good framework is started.

Authorities suggest the following general treatment for better fruit:

a. Dwarfing the plant by repressing wood growth hastens the fruiting period.

b. Root pruning.

c. Tying down branches below a horizontal position.

d. The removal of some foliage in summer.

These suggestions may help for better fruit production, but the climate, soil conditions and the varieties of the fruit are the first things to consider. Once the response of a plant within a district is known, then specific inducers for fruit promotion may be attempted. One should, however, even then be very conservative; a slow and methodical procedure is always better than a harsh and radical departure from formal treatment.

SHAPES OF TREES

The form of the tree is of great importance in fruit-tree culture. In America, the trees are kept low; such a size makes for easier and faster picking. Low-headed trees are considered best for commercial fruit growing. If, however, the lowest branch is too close to the ground, culture underneath the tree is difficult and the fruit borne on such a limb

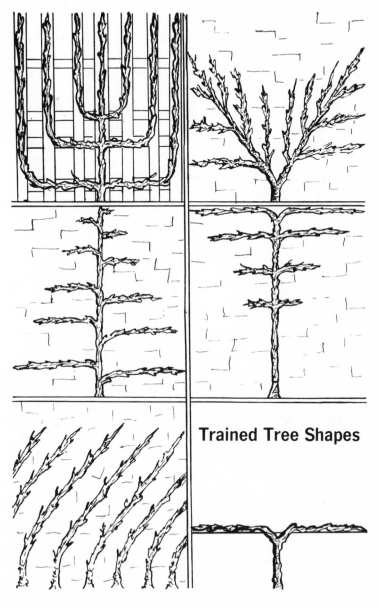

Trained Tree Shapes

is usually of a low grade. In Europe, fruit culture is more elaborate. Trees are permitted to grow taller and their life span is extended 2 to 5 times longer than in America. Many special modes of training are also practiced in the Old World, the result of ancient garden culture and patient hand-work. These methods are not practical for commercial fruit growing. These formal types of training with special supports are of 2 kinds: espaliers in which the plants are trained on cordons, horizontal, oblique, and fan-shaped structures; and the second group is trained on walls in similar shapes to those listed under the espaliers. These types are of only horticultural interest in formal gardens, but not for practical orchard culture.

THE OPEN CENTER TYPE OF TREE

In the illustration on page 97 a typical open center types is demonstrated. In this open form 3 too many main branches arise from the same level from the trunk of the tree. This type of tree is considered very bad by many, since it induces severe crowding of the branches and unnecessary competition among them. There is also the chance of a bad crotch development. This type of tree-form is usually the result of pruning old and neglected orchard trees, a condition that cannot always be corrected; it often necessitates the use of props and braces. We have mentioned that this umbrella type of pruning is ideal for some shade trees but it is rarely advisable for fruit trees.

SEMI-PYRAMID TYPE OF FRUIT TREE

Almost all of the species of economic fruit trees tend to have a naturally spreading vase shape in their outline. This type, however, is rather close in form to the open center shape which we have condemned as not the best, particu-

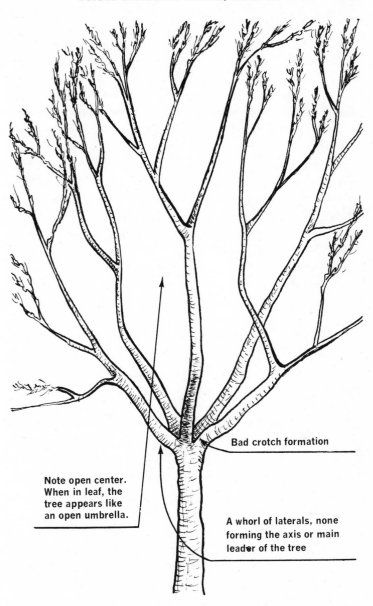

Bad crotch formation

Note open center. When in leaf, the tree appears like an open umbrella.

A whorl of laterals, none forming the axis or main leader of the tree

larly from a mechanical, structural point of view. The partly semi-pyramidal tree has a central leader and several subleaders, never more than 6. They are distributed vertically and radiate from the central trunk of the tree at various distances from each other, but the central leader is never obscured, being always most dominant and conspicuous as the central axis of the tree which should carry the major mechanical support of the mechanical strength of the tree. After the tree has reached a desired height, the leader's upward growth is checked. The tree may then be topped, always by cutting back to a point above a vigorous lateral that will become the new leader. By this type of care the contour of the tree is not vase shaped but suggests a pyramid in outline with one dominant axis and several subordinate leaders that will aid in widening the tree. If lateral leaders tend to become too dominant and crowd the selected leader, the pruner should hold these aggressive laterals in check. At times the upper branches may become too vigorous and out-grow the lower ones and may even make these latter ones weak; if that happens, the upper branches must be checked back by pruning.

SPACING OF BRANCHES

The distance of branches, one from the other, varies in species of fruit trees. We have mentioned the seriousness of branches that arise opposite to within 4 inches of each other from the trunk. These close branches may choke out the central leader. If this happens it may decay and the rot may so weaken the trunk that it may split eventually. If the leader dies, one of the opposite laterals may become the leader, but we have learned the possible consequence of a stub branch. The original leader cannot help leaving a stump; its rot will eventually weaken the new leader and

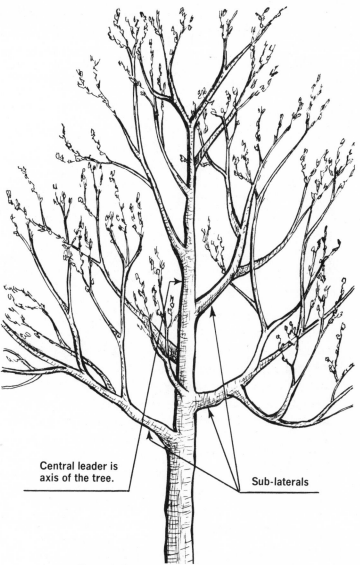

Central leader is
axis of the tree.

Sub-laterals

Semi-Pyramid-Shaped Tree

[99]

the remaining limb that was originally opposite, since the stump is between them both. The ideal space between lateral branches is from 6 to 8 inches. This can be achieved only in the early care of the tree when the framework is planned by the pruner.

TRAINING AND PRUNING THE 1-YEAR OLD WHIP

A 1-year old whip is a plant possessing no side branches or laterals. This whip treelet should be of a good height when set out; undersized plants are more difficult to handle. Do not cut back the tip when planting, but after growth is well established in early summer, selection of the main branches is made, with the laterals at a proper distance from each other. Always note the angles of the crotch in making the selection. The framework of the tree is started at this period.

PRUNING 2-YEAR OLD STOCK

A 2-year old plant, primarily of Apple, Pear, Cherry, or Plum, usually has several laterals developed. These laterals are often too close together and may be injured and broken in shipping and, in general, do not bear fruit any quicker than a 1-year old whip after setting out. It is often necessary to cut out all but 2 to 4 laterals to leave sufficient space between them for a good framework. We recommend the use of 1-year old stock as best for setting out; since the pruning is then confined to pinching out and rubbing off instead of cutting through wood with clippers; there is much less chance of injury.

CARE OF A TREE STARTED WITH
A GOOD FRAMEWORK

Once the tree is shaped properly with a good leader and well angled laterals, properly distanced, pruning care

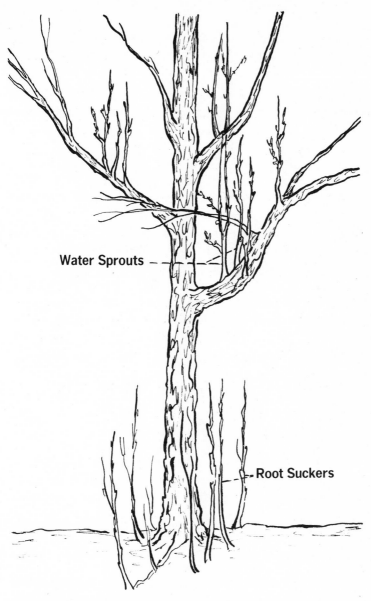

Water Sprouts

Root Suckers

should be very light until the tree begins to bear fruit. The pruning should be limited to preserving and assuring the established framework of the original training and selection. Real damage is often done during this period by over pruning; if in doubt, do not prune. Heavier pruning, however, is begun once the tree is bearing fruit. At this time undesirable growth is checked or cut out. To keep the inner branches of the tree healthy and vigorous, some sunlight must penetrate through the upper part of the plant. Otherwise, the excessive-shaded lower branches will die, as we have learned with trees in general. The pruner can easily distinguish branches that produce high grade fruit and those that fail to bear or produce only inferior fruit; these latter branches should be noted and removed later by the pruner. As a rule the older the tree, the more severe the pruning. Root suckers that sprout up at the base of the tree are often the result of too deep cultivation, whereby the surface roots have been cut or injured; these sprouts arise adventitiously from the cut roots. They should all be removed since they are never of value; in most cases they are shoots of the stock graft, and naturally this type of growth must always be suppressed.

WATER SPROUTS OR SUCKERS

Water sprouts are often a nuisance and will choke and crowd the tree if permitted to grow. They are more prevalent with cultured plants than with plants found in nature. They arise most readily near large wounds caused by pruning, having their origin from adventitious buds. They also seem to arise most readily on the shaded part of the trunk of vigorous growing trees; thus, they grow extremely fast through any available opening to get to the light, resulting in long, thin, spindly shoots. As a rule, they should all be removed unless there is an opening in the tree into which a new branch is desired. Naturally, selection should be made of suckers near the top of the tree; those in the middle and on the lower part of the tree are usually not of value. Suckers, in general, should be removed during summer months by jerking them out by hand while they are still soft; cutting them with clippers may often induce more to develop from possible basal and lateral buds on the shoot. We call them suckers because they suck out the vitality of the tree and give very little in return.

Root suckers threaten the vitality of a tree and should be removed.

Chapter Six

SPECIFIC CLASSES OF PLANTS

PRUNING SHRUBS

Many species of shrubs do not require regular pruning and are often much more attractive if left to grow naturally. They are pruned, however, when they tend to outgrow the space originally given to them. When pruning is necessary it is done by two distinct methods, the different shrub species being classed into two major groups.

I. The shrubs in the first group are pruned merely by thinning out and slightly cutting back or shortening new growth. This type of pruning is applied to shrubs that flower from wood matured the previous year. In this group, pruning should follow as soon as the blooming period is over.

II. The second group consists of those plants or shrubs that are to be pruned severely by cutting back and thinning out the branches. This group consists of those flowering shrubs that bear their flowers from shoots of the current year. These shrubs should be pruned in late autumn or toward the end of February.

These two different groups of flowering shrubs can easily be identified. If the flowers develop on the previous year's growth, like the Lilacs, they belong to group I; if the flowers develop on new wood like that of the Hydrangea species, they belong to group II.

The average man, however, finds a normal urge to prune in the spring. He is certain to note his shrubs. He reasons that something should be cut out. Before cutting, by all means clean out the leaves from under the shrubs;

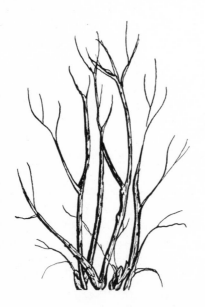

Severe Pruning of Hydrangea

[106]

they harbor slugs, grubs and many wintering insects. Use the clippers; they are bound to be many dead shoots which should be removed from the shrubs. Bushes in general should be kept open so that the branches may receive full benefit of light and air. Many species have numerous young root shoots like the Lilac. These will not bloom during the season and in many species not for many years, since the shoots must have a definite maturity before its young growth can bear flowers. These sucker shoots can be removed since they are usually unsightly and take away a great deal of strength and nourishment from the plant. It is wise to cut out most of them, leaving only a few that may be used in later years to replace older and injured flower-

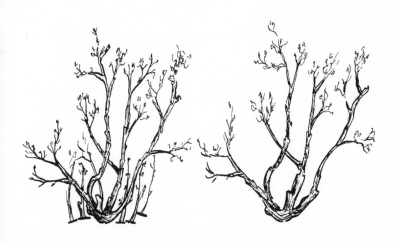

Slight Pruning of Syringa

[107]

ing branches. It is often advisable to remove a few of the older branch shoots, to the ground if possible, since this technique tends to invigorate the health of the shrub and keep it "young." In removing a branch or cane or stem from the shrub, it is best to cut it out close to the ground and protect the wounds if large. The shrub should have a drooping, spray-like appearance. Cutting branches half way makes a stubby appearance. The expert pruner will cut shrubs in such a way that, when he has completed the task, the shrub appears trim and does not show ugly traces of his pruning. The branches left should droop over and cover all the points of removal. There are exceptions to this rule, since some shrubs border drive-ways or are planted along walks. Elongated branches become a nuisance to cars passing through the drive-way, or to people who may be whipped by branches, particularly in rainy or snowy weather. Do not stub the shrub back only a few feet; the blunt ends not only cause scratching and injury but they give an unsightly form to the shrub. The flowering habits of a variety should be well known before one attempts to prune. In the following list of the most common flowering shrubs, suggestions for their specific treatment are given. Only the genus name is listed, indicating that the species under it are treated alike. Exceptions will be noted.

ABELIA

Remove old flower-heads and thin the plant out occasionally. The shrub needs no regular pruning. The species are not fast growing, have small graceful leaves, and attractive clusters of flowers.

AMELANCHIER   *Service Berry, Shad-bush, Juneberry*

No specific pruning is necessary.

ANDROMEDA   *Bog-Rosemary*

Evergreen shrubs often used in formal gardens and perennial borders. No specific pruning required.

ARBUTUS   *Madrona, Strawberry Tree*

Ornamental woody plants with handsome evergreen foliage and attractive flowers and fruits. No special pruning is essential.

ARCTOSTAPHYLOS   *Manzanita, Bearberry*

Ornamental evergreen shrubs and some species of trailing plants with attractive flowers and fruits. Very little pruning is required.

ARTEMESIA   *Wormwood*

Shorten the previous year's growth in February to prevent the plant from becoming straggly. Old wood can be removed without injury and plants can be shaped as desired.

BAMBOO

Various kinds of hardy varieties should be pruned every year, April being the best month. Never shorten a shoot; it will become stiff and ugly in appearance. Leaves that turn yellow during the summer may be removed without injury to the plant. Always cut out old shoots to the ground when removing them; short stubs crowd and injure the development of new shoots from the rhizomes.

BERBERIS   *Barberry*

Most of the common species do not require regular pruning. except the Oregon Grape (Mahonia) when grown as a ground cover; it should be cut back after the flowers fade, clipping in such a manner that the cuts are not visible but covered by some foliage. A uniform shearing would be unsightly.

BUDDLEIA   *Butterfly-Bush, Summer Lilac*

Some of the species have a more attractive, bushy appearance when longer branches are shortened; other species should be pruned severely each year for the best results. Cut back the previous year's growth to within a few buds of its base in February and thin out the young shoots as soon as they are large enough to pinch.

BUXUS   *Box*

No regular pruning is necessary. Hedge effects may be cut during the summer. Box, used in topiary work, should be clipped twice during the summer.

CALLICARPA   *Beauty Berry*

These shrubs of attractive fall berries should be thinned out when necessary, retaining as much young wood as possible, though shortening the points or tips.

CALYCANTHUS   *Sweet-scented Shrub, Sweet Shrub,*
                               Carolina Allspice, Strawberry Shrub

No regular pruning is needed.

CAMELLIA

This beautiful ornamental and colorful flowering genus, particularly *Camellia japonica* with its hundreds of hybrids, needs no regular pruning, though it should be cut back moderately when it becomes overgrown.

CARAGANA   *Pea Tree, Pea Shrub*

These beautiful shrubs are becoming most popular for their delicate and attractive, sweat-pea-like, yellow flower clusters. No pruning is required when the shrub is mature, but young plants need shaping.

CEANOTHUS

There are many colorful hybrids and varieties of this genus which is divided into two distinct groups in reference to pruning. One group consists of shrubs grown as bush plants which require very little care other than keeping them well balanced and with open centers. The other group includes the summer and early flowering species, varieties, and the many hybrids of *Ceanothus americanus*. Blooms develop on new shoots of the season's growth. Cut back the flowering shoots of the previous year in February. A strong shoot may be cut back to within 9 to 12 inches; weak ones to within 1 to 2 buds. Also remove old wood permitting a new root shoot to replace it.

CELASTRUS   *Bittersweet*

These climbing shrubs need no regular pruning when plants have plenty of room. Where the space is limited or restricted, thin out and shorten the branches in February.

CERCIS   *Judas Tree*

Shape the plants when young, but prune as little as possible when the plant is mature, removing only dead wood.

CISTUS   *Rock-Rose*

Pruning is not required, but remove old flower heads as soon as the bloom is completed.

CLEMATIS

When grown where there is ample room for development, many may be grown without pruning, except for clipping

[111]

off the dead ends of the branches after the end of the flowering period or at the end of February. Trained against walls and trellises, they require more pruning to keep the plants in bounds. Some species should be cut back in February to within a few buds of the previous year's growth; others must not be pruned until after the flowers have faded, and even then the pruning should be very light. Early flowering forms should not be pruned until after the flowering period, but late summer and early autumn varieties may be pruned in February, or before early spring.

CLERODENDRON *Glory-Bower*

As a rule they do not need regular pruning, but *Clerodendron speciosissimum* gives the best results if cut to the ground each spring.

CLETHRA *White Alder, Sweet Pepper Bush*

No special pruning is needed.

CNEORUM *Spurge-Olive*

No regular pruning is required.

CORNUS *Dogwood*

All the species can be successfully grown without specific pruning. Overgrown plants may be cut back severely without injury, and the many kinds grown for the colored bark for winter color may be cut to the ground in the spring. The "Flowering Dogwood" is treated as a small tree.

CORYLOPSIS *Winter Hazel*

These species with their fragrant attractive yellow spring flowers need no regular pruning.

COTONEASTER

These beautiful shrubs of deciduous and evergreen leaves are small and attractive and their small apple-like blossoms need no specific pruning. Their branches spread gracefully in horizontal positions in all directions.

CRATAEGUS   *Hawthorn, Thornapple*

Many of the species are tree-like; others are most shrubby. No special pruning is needed.

CYDONIA   *Quince*

When grown as bushes they require no pruning. If grown as a hedge it may be cut back when the flowering period is over.

CYTISUS   *Broom*

Prune each year after the blooming period is over, but do not cut beyond the base of the previous year's wood. Unpruned plants soon become ragged and sprawling.

DAPHNE

These beautiful flowering shrubs are always a source of attraction; they need no specific pruning.

DEUTIZIA

These common shrubs with white, bluish or purplish flowers should be thinned out well once in three years by removing as much of the old wood as possible. The best time for this pruning is in early summer.

DIERVILLA   *Bush-Honeysuckle,* likewise *Weigela*

Two methods of pruning are suggested: either the bushes may be allowed to develop naturally with the removal of

[113]

older wood about once every third or fourth year, thus keeping the shrub young; or the plant may be trained to form only a few rather short main branches by cutting the secondary branches on which the flowers develop. This should be done each year as soon as the flowers fade. The branches should be cut back to strong young shoots below the flowers. This latter type of pruning results in exceptionally good-flowering shrubs, but this treatment decreases the life span of the shrub.

ELAEAGNUS *Oleaster, Silverberry, Buffalo Berry*

These silvery-leaved shrubs are always an attraction and in general do not require regular pruning, except to curb straggling habits of growth by shortening the longest shoots during the summer. Green-leaved shoots that often appear among the variegated varieties should be removed as soon as they are observed.

ENKIANTHUS

These plants are attractive, particularly for their autumn colored leaves. No special pruning is required.

ERICA *Heath*

The taller species require no special pruning care except to remove loose growth when it appears; this is removed after the blooming period. The dwarf species are improved by removing all the old flower heads as soon as they fade.

ESCALLONIA

When used as shrubs they require no special treatment but when grown against walls or used as a hedge the shrubs should be cut back each year, after the flowers have faded.

EUONYMUS   *Spindle Bush, Straberry Bush, Wahoo*

Most of the species need no pruning. *Euonymus japonicus* requires a little shaping when grown as a shrub, but treated as a hedge it should be clipped once or twice during the summer. *Euonymus radicans,* grown normally as ground cover under trees or as a border for beds, should be trimmed or cut over either in spring or summer.

FICUS   *Fig*

If it is grown as an ornamental, thin out the branches occasionally and shape the bush, doing this in February.

FORSYTHIA   *Golden Bells*

Special pruning is not necessary for many of the species, except for thinning out every third year; or they may be clipped moderately each year, as soon as the flowering period is over, particularly *Forsythia suspensa.* When the plants are grown against a wall or a trellis, the secondary branches may be cut back to within a few buds of their base. When grown as a bush, the main branches should be allowed to grow 2 to 3 feet high, and the secondary branches should be cut back to that height each year. This method stimulates the formation of long shoots during the summer which will be in full bloom from end to end the following spring. This results in a controlled shrub of a definite height from year to year.

FOTHERGILLA

These attractive shrubs need no special pruning.

FREMONTIA CALIFORNICA   *Flannel-Bush*

This American evergreen species is becoming popular as a flowering shrub. The longest branches may be cut back in the spring, but severe pruning is not recommended.

[115]

FUCHSIA

The younger branches should be cut back to within two buds of their base. Branches that have suffered "winter-kill" should be cut back to the ground in February.

GAULTHERIA   *Wintergreen*

A few of the species are used as ground cover under shade in rock gardens. No pruning is required.

GAYLUSSACIA   *Huckleberry*

They are often used as ornamentals in bird sanctuaries since the fruit is an attraction for birds. No pruning is needed.

GENISTA   *Broom*

Treat the same as Cytisus, except the large growing species; these do not need regular pruning after they have developed good bushy formations.

GORDONIA   *Loblolly Bay*

These attractive shrubs need no formal pruning.

HALESIA   *Silver-Bell, Snowdrop Tree*

These plants can be treated as trees or shrubs. A little thinning may be required if the species are grown as shrubs.

HAMAMELIS   *Witch-Hazel*

Prune only to shape the plants, particularly when they are young; older plants have no need of further formal pruning. Some of the oriental species become very tall, averaging 30 feet in height.

[116]

HEDERA   *Ivy*

Ivy grown in the form of a bush may require a little shaping each year, merely removing a branch here and there. Old, straggling plants may be invigorated by cutting back in spring. If grown against walls, Ivy should be cut back as close as possible to the walls in February or March; these hanging branches may become too heavy with new growth and tend to pull away from the wall in heavy winds and storms. At the same time cut back the upper shoots well below the roof or gutters if the Ivy is grown on the side wall of a home. One should also examine and cut the plants toward the beginning of July, removing long shoots that are protruding away from the wall.

HELIANTHEMUM   *Sun-Rose*

These border rock-garden woody plants, often used as ground cover, should have their attractive flowers removed as soon as they fade.

HIBISCUS   *Rose Mallow*

No formal pruning is required, particularly with *Hibiscus syriacus,* the "Rose-of-Sharon" of gardens.

HYDRANGEA

A few species of Hydrangea require very little pruning other than an occasional thinning and the removal of old flower heads. The popular species most grown in gardens have a definite formal pruning. *Hydrangea macrophylla* (*H. HORTENSIS*) should have the older shoots thinned out, but do not shorten the young shoots. There are many varieties and colors of this species. *Hydragnea arborescens* and its varieties such as "Hills-of-Snow" should be pruned rather severely in February, removing old shoots entirely and short-

[117]

ening the previous season's growth to a length of 9 to 12 inches. *Hydrangea paniculata* and its popular variety *grandiflora,* may be pruned in February by removing the old flower head and cutting out weak shoots, or the shrub may be pruned a little more severely. The severe pruning means the removal of some of the older shoots and the shortening of the previous season's wood to within two eyes of the base. In the spring thin out a few of the new shoots, thus limiting the number of branches; this method of control stimulates the formation of very large inflorescences. However, this type of pruning should accompany a generous compost treatment to the roots, since shrubs treated severely and growing in poor soil would be very unsuccessful. *Hydrangea radiata* may be pruned similar to *Hydrangea arboresens.* The climbing species, *Hydrangea petiolaris,* when grown against a wall, should be cut back after flowering, but if grown over a tree stump or over some other support, it needs no pruning.

HYPERICUM   *St. Johnswort*

In general, thin out the older wood of the taller species each year and shorten the previous year's shoots. The dwarf form, *Hypericum calycinum,* should be cut back to within an inch or two of the ground. The "Golden-Flower," *Hypericum Moserianum,* should be thinned out and the remaining shoots shortened about half way each year. All pruning is best done in February, or in very early spring.

ILEX   *Holly*

Do not clip back the shoots since they are naturally stiff and most erect; instead clean out some of the laterals of the shoots thus accentuating them. All green-leaved shoots should be removed from variegated varieties. Holly hedges may be clipped back in the middle or end of summer.

ITEA VIRGINICA   *Sweet Spire*

Older shoots should be thinned out and the younger ones should be shortened in February. *Itea ilicifolia* may be pruned in the same manner.

JASMINUM   *Jasmine Jessamine*

The bushy species require occasional thinning but no other formal treatment. *Jasminum nudiflorum* and *Jasminum primulinum* should have the flowering shoots cut back to within two buds of the base as soon as the flowers fade, but no further pruning should follow.

KALMIA   *Lambkill, Mountain Laurel*

The species have no need of formal pruning.

KERRIA JAPONICA

This species with its many horticultural varieties should have much of its older wood removed to encourage vigorous young wood. Prune as soon as the flowers fade; the previous year's wood should be slightly shortened after thinning out and the removal of old wood.

LAURUS   *Bay, Laurel, Sweet Bay*

Formal pruning is not required other than shaping if necessary. This should be done during the summer. Overgrown plants may be severely pruned in April. Tub plants should be carefully clipped two or three times a summer.

LAVANDULA   *Lavender*

Cut below the flower stalks soon after blooming or during late winter. If more severe pruning is necessary, it would be best done in March.

[119]

LEDUM   *Wild Rosemary, Labrador-Tea, Crystal-Tea*

This genus of evergreen shrubs, often used for border plants, requires no special pruning.

LEUCOTHOE

Often used as ornamentals. Plants treated as shrubs should have their older stems removed and the younger shoots shortened in late February before the spring season arrives. Shrubs grown for the color effect of their bright green barks should be cut close to the ground in March.

LIGUSTRUM   *Privet*

Shrubs need no special pruning, but hedges should be clipped several times during the summer. They tolerate severe abuse.

LIPPIA

Species of this genus with spikes and heads of white, rose, or purplish flowers need no regular pruning.

LONICERA   *Honeysuckle*

The true shrub species should be thinned out every three to four years, and if overgrown, the longer shoots should be cut back; this pruning is done best in summer, but do not prune every year. The climbing species require very little formal pruning if they have room to develop; but if the plants are growing under restricted conditions, they may be cut after the flowering period.

LYONIA (XOLISMA)

These white and pinkish flowering shrubs need no specific pruning care.

MAGNOLIA

The shrubby species do not require regular pruning.

MENISPERMUM *Moonseed*

These climbers should be cut back in February or early March, removing ragged growth.

MYRICA *Bayberry, Sweet Gale, Wax-Myrtle*

No formal pruning is necessary.

MYRTUS *Myrtle*

Other than a little shaping, no regular pruning is required, unless these ornamental shrubs are growing near a wall or fence, in which case they may need cuting back. This is best done in March.

NERIUM *Oleander*

No specific pruning is necessary.

PACHYSANDRA

These evergreen subshrubs, often used most successfully as ground cover under very shady conditions, need no special pruning.

PAEONIA SUFFRUTICOSA *Moutan*

This woody species of Peony, with its many varieties, should have its dead tips clipped off from the ends of the branches; no other pruning is required.

PASSIFLORA *Passion Flower*

The secondary branches of these climbers should be cut back to within a few buds of the base of the branches, doing this during the winter or early spring. Also replace old wood with young shoots when possible.

PHILADELPHUS *Mock Orange*

The greater number of the species of this genus needs no formal pruning. In fact, they are best if left untouched; thin out a little at intervals of a few years. The hybrids of *Philadelphus Lemoinei,* however, respond best when all the flowering shoots are removed as soon as the flower fade, cutting back to vigorous shoots that have not bloomed. Some of the old flowering shoots may sometimes be removed to the ground. The new vigorous shoots will bloom from end to end. The cutting out of the old shoots must not be delayed after the flowers have faded, for the success of the pruning depends on a long growing and formative season.

PIERIS

No formal pruning is necessary other than the removal of the old faded flowers.

RHAMNUS *Buckthorn*

No special pruning is required.

RHODODENDRON (includes AZALEAS)

The majority of Rhododendrons need no regular pruning except for the removal of the flower heads as soon as the flower fades. However, young plants should be clipped occasionally to induce a sturdy habit. Overgrown plants that are old may be cut back severely without serious injury but this should be done in March or April.

RHUS *Sumac*

When grown for the large compound leaves and autumn coloration the young shoots must be cut down to within a few inches of the ground in February or early March. If the plants are grown for shrubbery, no special pruning is required.

RIBES *Flowering Currants and Gooseberries*

No special pruning is required.

ROBINIA

The shrubby *Locusts* should be cut back a little in summer to prevent the branches from becoming too long and rank in appearance.

ROSA *Rose*

There are many methods advocated for pruning Roses. Some species are best left entirely alone if the shrubs have ample room. Ramblers and Climbers should have all the old flowering canes removed as soon as the flowers fade; the new canes developing during the summer will bloom the next season. Bush roses should have all the weak wood removed, and vigorous young canes from the root should be encouraged. Some cut these canes from 6 to 8 inches high; other authorities advise leaving them a little taller. Always take the opportunity to remove old wood when it can be replaced by a young cane. Some have the bush effect a definite height and cut young laterals arising from the older wood, to two eyes. It is advisable to cut back to an outer eye to permit the shoot from the eye to have plenty of room to grow away from the center of the plant. This general pruning is best done in March. One can also aid the plant when cutting flowers for bouquets: cut back to good eyes, thus a bit of pruning is exercised.

ROSMARINUS OFFICINALIS *Rosemary*

No special pruning is necessary.

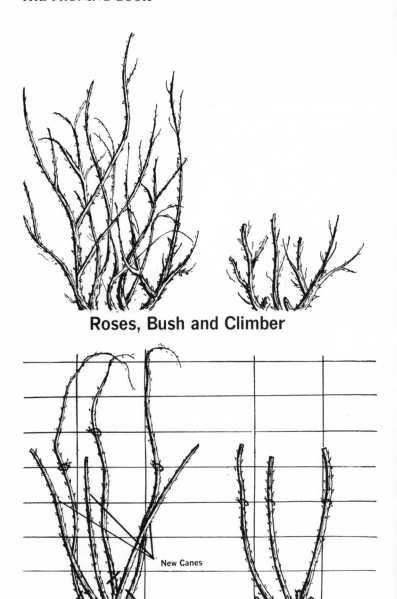

Roses, Bush and Climber

New Canes

SALIX   *Willows*

If grown for colored bark effects, cut them back to within a few eyes of the crown in March.

SAMBUCUS   *Elder*

If grown for colored foliage, cut it to the ground in February, otherwise no regular pruning is required.

SPIRAEA   *Spirea*

The major group of the species needs very little pruning. *Spiraca thunbergii* and some others may be slightly "winter-killed" on the tips; these injured shoots should be removed. The spring flowering species such as *Spiraea prunifolia, Spiraea Vanhouttei,* and *Spiraea crenata* may be pruned after blooming. The summer-flowering species such as *Spiraea Bumalda, Spiraea Billiardii,* and *Spiraea tomentosa* may be pruned lightly in spring to stimulate flower-bearing shoots.

STAPHYLEA   *Bladder Nut*

No special pruning is necesary.

STEPHANDRA INCISA

Often used as a low hedge plant. It may be thinned out every second year if used as a shrub.

SYRINGA   *Lilac*

If the plants are flowering freely no regular pruning in any form is needed. If the shrubs are not flowering well and growth is weak, thin out the branches, removing some of the inside wood and the weak shoots in April. Inspect the shrubs again early in June and remove the weaker shoots; this concentrates the energy on building up the remaining

[125]

wood. In any case, all suckers should be removed from the base of the plant at least once a year. They are unsightly and consume energy from the plant.

TAMARIX   *Tamarisk*

When grown as hedges or as dwarf plants, prune them as soon as the flowers fade. Plants grown naturally need no specific pruning.

VIBURNUM

No special pruning is required.

VINCA   *Periwinkle*

Formal pruning is not necessary, though *Vinca major* may be cut back occasionally.

WISTARIA

To control this climber and have shrub-like plants, shorten the young shoots back to within 5 to 6 of its basal buds in July, and shorten back to 2 to 3 buds in winter. As an extensive climber, it does not require special pruning.

Chapter Seven

HOW TO PRUNE
A HEDGE

OF ALL PLANTINGS near a home, the hedge is the most neglected. The average individual will admit that a hedge requires care, but he confesses his neglect. If it grows too tall or too wide he merely clips out the inconvenience, and the poor hedge must struggle on the best it can. It may never be cultivated, cleaned out, or fed a dressing of compost. No wonder individual plants of the hedge die out making bad spots, when the caught, dead leaves and debris blown in by the wind snag at the base of the hedge plants until it rots. Uncover some of this snagged material, wet paper, partly rotted leaves, the dead branches at the base of the hedge, and note the myriads of eggs of insects, and spore plants of fungi; it is a pest hole of many of the garden enemies, all comfortably established in the nursery of the well-protected base of the neglected hedge. I have counted thousands of slug eggs and other insect larvae early in the spring that would feed at the base of the plants and finally swarm out and become the normal pests of a garden. If anyone complains about the poor results of his flower or vegetable garden, note the condition of the base of his hedges. Thus, the first step with every hedge is to clean it out by removing the dead wood and leaves within its center, to cultivate the soil and feed, and finally to remove all plants that do not belong within the hedge; they are all weeds. I have found seedling Maples, Rose of Sharon, English Ivy, strangling Bind Weed, Barberry plants, Poison Ivy, Virginia Creeper, Elms, and many other that are weeds when growing within a hedge planting. In fact I counted 40 species of "squatters" within a 50 foot hedge of Privet. After removing all of the dead and broken branches of the hedge one then tackles the hedge itself.

A hedge is often a problem for the pruner, particularly if it has not been properly trained or has been given a good start, but then neglected. Often the hedge is old, has bad dead spots, is "leggy" or has outgrown its originally planned objective. What is the remedy? A pruner often finds the remedy by simply pruning out bad conditions, cultivating, giving a good dressing of compost, or if it is too badly diseased and in bad condition, by digging up the plants and resetting them. Starting a new hedge may be advisable with new young plants; then we can use the older selected plants that may be salvaged for a different type of hedge. A hedge is normally a single row of plants of a specific species, planted closely together and equally full of foliage from the top to the bottom; it should be widest at the base. It may serve as:

> 1. A border or edging in formal gardening; these are normally low to divide the garden into sections. This type is classed as ornamental.

2. Boundary lines for property, as a practical indicator; thus, a service hedge.

3. Guards along walks and lanes to protect a lawn or a flower bed and as a precaution against careless visitors another form of low, ornamental type.

4. A high screen effect to assure privacy for certain areas, a service type.

5. Wind-breaks to protect many types of plantings, barns, and even homes; thus, a form of service.

6. Defensive borders to prevent trespassing and intrusion, eliminating the use of unsightly wire and wooden fences; this may be classed as both ornamental and service.

These types must be kept in mind and properly interpreted before a pruner begins the next step of pruning. The beauty and value of a hedge is in its thickness or density of growth and in its general uniformity from end to end and top to bottom. The pruner must know the specific limits of the species. There are two general classes of formal hedges: those that survive shearing 2 to 3 times a season, and those that do not respond to more than 1 shearing or none at all, but react well to pruning. Let us assume the pruner is planning to set out a new hedge.

PRIMARY PRUNING OF A NEW HEDGE

For planting a hedge the soil should be well prepared and dressed with a rich compost. A trench is dug and all large stones removed to assure drainage. The trench is dug 2 feet deep and 2 feet wide and filled with mixed top-soil and compost. The plants are then set in a single row, never in a double row, and each plant is placed at least 2 to 3 inches deeper than the soil-line indicated on the stem near

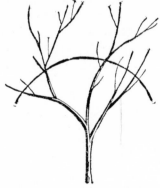

A—Cut back new plant

B—Wrong shape—flat top

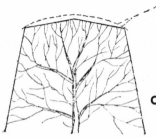

top rounded or angled

C—Correct—base widest

the roots. The plants should be set close together, if a dense type of hedge is desired. The formal low, or 1 foot high type of hedge, should have the plants 4 inches apart or less; hedges 3 to 4 feet in height should have the plants set 6 inches apart. If the hedge is to be informal or unclipped, the plants may set further apart. All the deciduous species or plants that drop their leaves in the fall should be cut back severely as shown in fig. A on page 130. In the case of Privet or Barberry, the newly set plants should be cut back at least ⅓ of their length. We have learned under General Pruning Rules that topping causes lateral growth. This is the important type of response anticipated for hedges, the inducement of lateral branches close to the ground to prevent long, naked stems. It is a serious mistake to permit young hedge plants to grow for a period before cutting back, since then there is less chance for the plants to make a full, dense growth of a branch system at the base. Planting time is the important period for preparing a hedge; the hedge will be either thin and skimpy if not cut back, or bushy and full if clipped. Evergreens, however, are often received in a ball of earth covered with burlap; these plants are not planted as closely as deciduous species, nor should they be clipped back so severely.

After the plants are planted and cut back, they should be clipped or sheared 2 or 3 times during the growing season. Each shearing should involve the removal of new growth 1 to 2 inches above the previous clipping. We have learned from pruning that excess cutting induces wood growth. In hedge-training this is the main objective, to have a great deal of new growth of as many side branches, branchlets and tiny twigs as possible. When there seems to be enough of this type of growth and the hedge has reached the desired height, as, in the case of the privet, when the

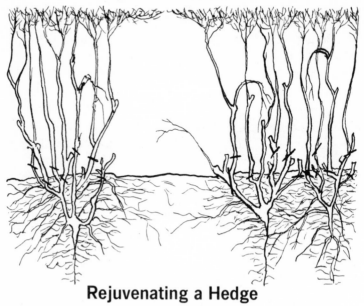

Rejuvenating a Hedge

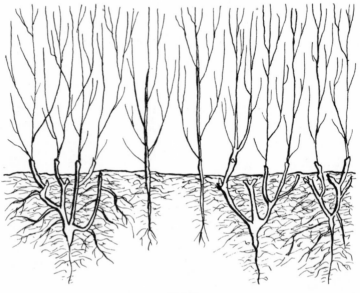

plants are 3 to 4 feet high, shearing is conducted in such a manner that the base will always be wider than the top of the hedge, as illustrated in the figs. B and C. Avoid if possible a flat top; have it either slightly rounded or angled; packed snow often injures the flat top type of a hedge.

CARE OF THE MATURE HEDGE

A properly trained hedge, once mature, should be pruned, cultivated and given a soil dressing annually, during the early spring. If formal, it should be sheared 2 to 3 times during the growing season, depending on the species; the Boxwood may be sheared 3 or more times safely during the season.

If the hedge is informal, that is, permitted to grow at random, and if full growth is allowed, then only annual pruning of broken, diseased and dead branches is required with cultivation and soil feeding. Hedges not clipped are those described as defensive, screen, and wind-break types. In the southwest United States and particularly in Mexico, columnar species of Cacti are planted as defensive hedges and allowed to grow as densely as growth permits. I have observed such absolutely impregnable hedges. Other species of this type used are the Trifoliate Orange, Honey Locust, species of Crabapple, and the Osage Orange, though the latter must be topped or thinned out to discourage its habit to form trees.

Different species of conifers, evergreens and deciduous plants are available for hedges, depending on the climate and region in which the hedge is to be planted. A great number of species may be used for hedges, but the majority of these do not survive shearing; hence, they may be used only for informal hedges. The choice of species for formal hedges is extremely limited, the best being the Privet, Boxwood, and the Japanese Barberry.

[133]

Here Manager Keck is shown making his second cut following the first undercutting.

Chapter Eight

SHADE TREES AND EVERGREENS

CARE OF SHADE TREES

THE CARE of shade trees is of importance because they are of ornamental significance. Trees line our streets, are used about our homes, and if they are not properly treated they would soon become unsightly monstrosities and even hazards. A good street tree should have, as an average, ⅓ of a clear trunk to ⅔ of a crown. This is a conservative average, since many species would not be applicable to the rule. Above all, there should be a clear view for drivers along streets, and this perhaps should be one of the governing factors for the height of the trunk. An ideal tree is one having a straight, well-defined central trunk with side branches regularly distributed around it and more or less subordinate to it. Park departments of large cities usually take the responsibility of street trees and, as a rule, follow

[135]

the pattern of a properly shaped tree to prevent accidents and to have the tree so shaped that it will withstand fierce storms and sudden bursts of wind without too much injury and danger. An isolated tree near a home has a crown that tends to develop laterally rather than vertically, spreading over a large area. The head of the tree should be well balanced, composed of a comparatively small number of main branches but furnished with numerous secondary branches and branchlets bearing healthy and abundant foliage. This type of tree should be trimmed at least once in 3 to 4 years, keeping the leader shoots clear of walls, thinning out branches when they are too dense, and gradually removing the lower branches. It is not wise to prune shade trees during the period when sap begins to flow most actively. Some trees if pruned during this period bleed freely, such as Birches, Elms, and Maples. There is little danger of bleeding, however, once the leaves have developed; thus, summer and early autumn is the most suitable time for most ornamentals. Flowering trees, such as the Horse Chestnuts, Catalpas, Laburnums and Magnolias may be pruned as soon as the flowers fall off. The trimmer should have one basic objective in mind; not only should he remove injured, diseased, and faulty branches, but he should strive to clean out the inside of the tree to give it an umbrella-like effect as he looks up into the tree from the trunk. This type of pruning permits a bit of light to seep through for lawns and flower beds. Umbrella-like pruning is not suitable for all species; they can not tolerate the sun on the ground near the base of the trunk. All species of Oaks are sensitive to excess inner pruning; they are best left alone except for the removal of dead, injured, and diseased limbs. Often one meets with "Stag-headed" crowns, a term applied to old trees with the upper branches naked and dead, towering

[136]

over branches of the middle of the tree that are still in good health. This dead crown should be removed, since the dead wood is the seat of boring beetles that thrive on dead wood. All such trees should either be pruned or destroyed because the boring insects multiply so rapidly that they will be the source of infection for other trees within the neighborhood. If the tree is not too badly injured it may survive. Lateral branches may eventually twist upward to fill out the crown, though this process may take a few years. All species do not respond to this treatment, Oaks and Elms survive best, while the Beeches and Birches are most sensitive to it, since they are short-lived trees. Soft-wooded trees such as the Horse Chestnuts, Willows and Poplars may be reduced in height and diameter if the trunk is healthy, but if the trunk is partly decayed it is best to remove the trees and begin with young plants.

The general rule for the care of shade trees, grown normally for their beautiful broad leaves, is to prune during the summer and early fall. Trees of this type are Oaks, Maples, Ashes, Sycamores or Planes, Elms, Willows, Sweet and Sour Gums, and the Tulips. Most of these need very little pruning, merely the removal of dead and dangerous branches, and the shaping of the trees to specific desires.

Flowering trees should normally be pruned after the blooming period. A few of these trees are the Horse Chestnuts, some Locusts, Laburnums, Flowering Dogwoods, Magnolias, Catalpas, Paulownias, and the flowering Cherries, Plums, and Apples.

Evergreens, such as the Evergreen Oaks, Pepper trees, and the Eucalyptus, should not be pruned much but merely cleaned out, removing the dead branches and diseased wood. Most of this group, however, can survive severe pruning by topping and shaping, but this must be done be-

[137]

fore the new growth of leaves develops. Conifers, such as Pines, Spruces, Firs, and Junipers, should never be trimmed. If they are crowded, move them to better locations. They have their natural pyramidal shape and always appear well formed. Removing the terminal shoot is serious since 2 or more laterals will become the leaders and the tree will lose its natural shape. If the lower lateral branches die back it is a sign that something is wrong. Either an insect or fungus condition must be present, or there is too much crowding by other trees near or over it. To cut laterals out makes the conifer appear naked. Arbor Vitae and some Hemlocks are used as hedges and are trimmed accordingly but their life is not long under these conditions, and if a few trees should die out of the hedge they would be difficult to replace. Junipers have been used in this manner but there are many other species of flowering shrubs that would serve this requirement much better.

TREATMENT OF EVERGREENS

The group of plants classed as evergreens in horticulture, whether trees or shrubs, are those that retain their green foliage from season to season; in other words, they do not shed their leaves all at one time, as is the case with deciduous plants. In many species the leaves remain on the trees and function some years. This is particularly true of the large group called the Conifers, of which the Pine, Spruce, and Fir are examples. The leaves or needles do eventually drop off, either because of old age, injury, crowding, or excess shade, thus making them useless as functioning tissue. An evergreen tree or shrub never appears naked as in the case of a Lilac or a deciduous Maple. Observe a healthy well-placed branch of a Pine or Spruce tree, calculate the age of the limb and note that needles appear on from 3 to 10-year-old wood. I have found needles on even older wood.

We, in the temperate zone, think of evergreens as the Conifers, and in many respects they are the most dominant in this zone, though it is surprising to note the number of evergreens we do have and use for winter color. The Rhododendrons, Kalmias, Box, and many others are given in the list of shrubs already described. In the tropics, the Conifers are not so plentiful, comparative to the general flora of that region; in that zone most plants are evergreen and naturally Palms are the best example.

TRANSPLANTING EVERGREENS

Pruning of all forms of evergreens has already been discussed, but a word should be added on transplanting these forms. The best period to transplant deciduous trees is during the fall when the leaves have dropped. Evergreens, on the other hand, never pass through a definite dormant period when transpiration is nil. The presence of their leaves always means a loss of water; thus transplanting is always serious. This is also true of deciduous plants if they are transplanted during active periods and when the leaves are still present. The following rules are generally applied to transplanting evergreens at any time and deciduous trees in the summer:

1. Transplant evergreens under wet conditions. This implies not only wet soil due to rain, or in the presence of rain, but during cloudy days. Wet conditions are naturally most prevalent in the spring in the temperate regions and during the rainy season of the tropics.

2. If the conditions are not wet naturally, make them so by excessive watering, filling the hole into which the plant is to be placed with water so that the soil is well satu-

rated, and also syringing or wetting the leaves of the plant to keep down transpiration. Doing this creates a humid atmosphere immediately around the plant and thus prevents withering.

3. If possible, never transplant in the heat of the day. The best time is preferably at twilight; the plant thus has the advantage of the cool of the evening or of a high humidity, giving the plant a period of adjustment before the heat of the following day strikes it. Some even cover the plant with a cheese-cloth to umbrella it against the drying blast of the sun. Often, in the tropics, young plants are planted in the shade of other plants as a protection.

4. Always ball the plant before transplanting. This is almost a universal rule for evergreens whether of the tropics or the temperate zones. The technique of making a ball of earth around the roots must be thoroughly understood before attempted. One close observation of the actual process in a nursery suffices for learning. Note that it is done while the soil is in fairly wet condition, so that it will not crumble away. The actual digging is performed during cloudy, foggy, or the cooler periods of the day. It is well to wrap burlap or sacking around the ball to hold it in position and to serve as a mulching device, since the bag can be kept wet and so aid the roots. Larger trees require an elaborate structural method best performed by professionals.

5. Special treatment is given to Conifers. Many methods are suggested, but all authorities emphasize the need of preparing a ball of the roots, wrapped in burlap The soil must be fairly solid or wet to make a ball, holding the roots as much as possible in an undisturbed condition. The remaining fibrous roots after the ball is made, supply the needs of the tree to a degree, but a great deal of arti-

ficial help must be given to the tree, since this water supply would not be sufficient for the tree to survive. Many ball the Conifer 2 to 3 seasons before actually transplanting, constantly keeping the ball moist, thus stimulating growth on the cut ends of the roots. Examine the ball at least once a month by boring a little hole into the ball to note development. If the ball is too small or with insufficient root-hair development, or too dry, the plant may grow only a few inches the first two or three years. If the ball is successful and the tree is responding well, it will be revealed by the activity of growing 6 or more inches a year, or half the normal annual growth of the species under natural conditions. Some species of Conifers have an ample supply of fibrous roots and survive readily under this treatment, like that of the White Pine which, paradoxically, will carry on with a comparatively small root system. Other species of Conifers are characterized with distinct tap-roots; if these tap-roots are cut, and they must be if the plants are to be transplanted, the chances of survival are low, unless the plants are constantly nursed with sufficient supplies of water, and are well protected with the wrapped burlap that serves as a mulch and holds the soil in place.

6. Conifers should not be transplanted in winter; the cold drying winds of the winter are just as serious as the desiccating, hot winds of summer since transpiration is always going on, though not as excessive in winter months as in summer. Many claim that there is no "best time" and that the time of planting is of minor importance. But they do warn, "If the ball is frozen solid and remains so for one or two months, exposed to dry winds, the top may dry out and die." If it is necessary to plant during the winter months, then the soil about the location where the tree is to be placed should be well mulched to prevent freezing;

[141]

and when the tree is planted, the excessive mulching should be continued, similar to midsummer planting.

7. The technique of preparing a ball is tedious and laborious, but to assure success and save a good Conifer by transplanting, the effort is worth the gain. The trench, preparatory to making the ball, should be much wider than the decided size of the ball. The size of the ball is based on the height or age of the tree; the general proportion of size to the tree is: a tree 8 to 10 feet high requires a 3 foot ball in diameter; a 15 foot tree needs a 4½ foot ball; and a 35 foot tree should have a ball 12 feet in diameter. The fibrous roots thus released from the soil should be wrapped around the ball. Naturally, heavy roots that will not bend will have to be cut but this must be done with a sharp cut and always at right angles. When the ball is finally made, and the fibrous roots are wrapped around it, the burlap is then placed around the ball. The advantage of this is that it assures more fibrous roots or the maximum amount under the adverse conditions. The wet burlap then serves as a source of moisture for the rootlets and stimulates the injured roots to form needed root hairs. After these are well formed the plant can then be planted.

Chapter Nine

ROOTS AND
ROOT PRUNING

A PRUNER must also have a correct understanding of the function of the root, both how it is influenced when pruned, and how it reacts when the aerial part of the plant is pruned. In many cases, the failure of the plant to respond properly after pruning may be traced to the roots. This is particularly true of newly transplanted plants. If leaves are formed on such a plant before new roots have developed, and the root system has been seriously pruned back or injured, the moisture of the stem is soon exhausted and the plant may die. In moving any plant one must leave it enough feeding roots to support top growth. Even though all the principles of pruning may have been observed in reference to the shoots, branches and stems, neglect of the roots will undo all the excellent work performed on the

[143]

plant. So we may well ask, what are roots? Roots may be considered as simply an extension of the stem branching under ground. The cambium of the stem, being continuous with that of the root, forms wood cells within and bark cells without. An old root usually shows concentric layers or rings similar to those observed in a cross section of a stem. Thus, the root is the subterranean tissue of the plant and has three major functions: to anchor the plant securely in the soil against high winds; to hold the soil in place and to prevent erosion; and thirdly, to assimilate water and soil salts from the soil to supply the needs of the aerial part of the plant. It is the younger roots with living bark that function as pumping stations for water and soil salts in solution for the plant. A plant, whether a small herb or a giant tree, needs mineral salts and water for living protoplasm or living tissue and for the leaves, for the basic process of making food through the phenomenon, photosynthesis.

HOW DOES WATER ENTER A PLANT?

The actual intake of the water in the root system is located at the extreme tips and ends of the tiny rootlets. If one were carefully to remove a small plant from the soil and to wash the dirt away from the roots, one could see that the extreme ends of the roots are terminated by tiny fibrous-appearing rootlets. If we examine a tiny rootlet closer, we note a small tip or root-cap that covers the end of the root-let and protects its growing point as it pushes forward into new regions for possible supplies. Immediately beyond this root-cap there is a series of fine hairs radiating from the sides of the rootlet, the youngest and shortest being near the cap, and becoming progressively longer as one follows these hairs backward, until one comes to an area where they are collapsed and finally withered and torn away. Root hairs do not absorb water like a sponge but by means of a physical process regulated by living substance. The water and dissolved soil salts pass through the wall of the root hairs by the process called osmosis, by means of the jelly-like substance called protoplasm within each root-hair, the living substance acting as a controlling membrane. The number of these root-hairs determines the size of the aerial part of the plant; if they are few, the stem is dwarfed, and conversely, if many, the plant is large, at least normal in size, since there is a definite balance between the root system and the aerial part of the plant. The fine assimilating root-hairs come into very intimate contact with the minutest soil particles which contain minerals and which are surrounded by films of soil-moisture that becomes available to the plant. Thus, there is a definite necessity for guarding the root-hair region of all plants, whether herbs, shrubs, or trees, from injury so far as is possible, particularly in transplanting.

SPECIFIC EFFECTS OF ROOT PRUNING

Removal of evergreens requires greater care than that of deciduous plants; the former have a constant presence of leaves which demand water; thus, root pruning must be at a minimum, as is the case of citrus fruits. Root pruning is sometimes resorted to as a check to rapid top growth, especially in young apple trees, and in general this technique encourages the development of flower buds instead of leaf buds. It is definitely a dwarfing process and is resorted to in the Orient and classed as a form of horticulture to develop miniature plants of a woody nature. One rule to learn is that many species of fruit trees, if root pruned about the first of August in the temperate zone, will be checked in further growth and tend to form flower buds during the fall;

[145]

they also appear to show a greater disposition to forming many more flowers during the blooming period the following spring.

CARE OF ROOT INJURY AND ROOT PRUNING

In digging out a plant, a large proportion of the rootlet system is cut off. Many systems of root pruning are advocated but there is one basic law to observe: all injured or diseased material should be removed and cut back to healthy tissue. All spade cuts and ragged tears should be cut smoothly and at right angles to the root, as illustrated in fig. 5 on page 149. Never make an oblique cut if it is possible to do otherwise, since this results in a larger wound, and it will take longer for the root callus to cover the injury. A smooth cut forms a callus quickly and serves as a healing process for the wound. A circular cut of all the roots, as shown in fig. 3, is very bad since the heart of the rootlet system has been removed and the thread-like ends from which new rootlets develop readily are lost. Some plants may not even survive this type of treatment. Correct pruning is illustrated in fig. 1. In this figure there is no excess pruning; injuries have been removed, and the main root system has been left intact.

Often large trees are prepared a season in advance for transplanting. A circular trench is dug around the tree; the average radial distance of the trench from the tree is based on the ratio of 6 inches to every 1 inch of diameter of the trunk of the tree. The general root system varies with different species; broad-leaved trees usually have a wide spreading root system, often close to the surface; while conifers are deep and not so spreading. Some species have deep tap roots, serving as excellent anchorage, others are shallow rooted. Main root branches should be cut smooth

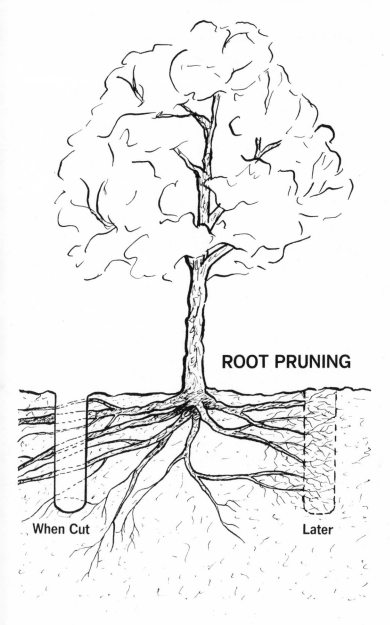

ROOT PRUNING

When Cut

Later

[147]

with a saw, not an axe. The trench is then closed and by the following spring a good supply of feeder roots will have started. The actual removal of the tree can then be done safely the following fall. In the northern United States some resort to heavy mulching of the transplanted trees to protect them from severe freezing and thawing, and to conserve moisture.

PRUNING TRANSPLANTED PLANTS

Some transplanted plants of certain species survive if the top is cut down to a pole, and the root system is cut back to a few feet from the trunk as illustrated in fig. 3. This severe treatment is possible with pear and peach trees since they produce new roots readily and have enough nourishment stored in the trunk to furnish food, consequently establishing the plant well before the hot weather comes. This severe treatment is, however, exceptional and cannot be recommended in general. On the other hand, many nut or ornamental trees, under such severe pruning, may either die immediately or succumb after a feeble struggle, within a few years.

The series of illustrations all show results of pruning the aerial part of a transplanted plant. In fig. 3 the plant has been cut to a pole. The exceptions to this type of pruning have been discussed and the method is discouraged. The result of this type of pruning is demonstrated in fig. 4. If the plant survives it will become scrubby with poor branch formation which may grow rank, in all directions. In fig. 1 the aerial part of the plant is pruned properly and is in balance with the root pruning. The result of this correct pruning is demonstrated in fig. 2. We must remember that the height of a fork of a trunk is fixed; it never grows higher; the branches do elongate, but not the base of the

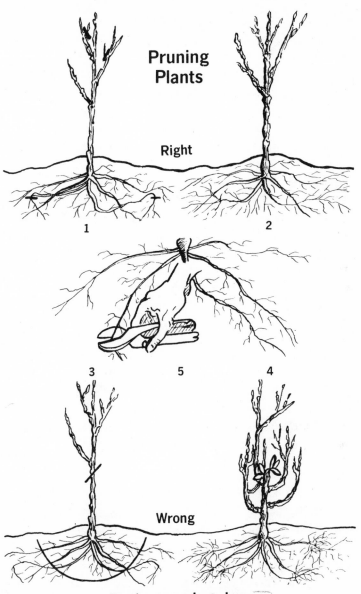

Pruning Plants

Right

1

2

3

5

4

Wrong

Pruning transplanted pears

[149]

branches, which grow only in thickness. Thus, in cutting off laterals, these factors must be considered.

The larger the tree, the greater will be the loss of the root system when the tree is moved. For the well-being of the transplanted tree, reduce the top proportionally in order to restore a balance; give the roots the benefit of the doubt and prune the aerial branches rather severely. Trees 3 to 5 years old, if lifted carefully, should be pruned back to within a few inches of the past year's growth; or you leave only a few buds of the seasons' growth. This assures reduced leaf surface and still preserves the original contour and ramification of the tree. Older and larger trees should be thinned out judiciously by removing a few larger branches, at the same time preserving the form of the top of the tree. Avoid as much as possible any appearance of heading back of old branches, which gives an unsightly effect to the outline of the tree. Trees, whether young or old, planted in the fall or as soon as they shed their leaves and become deciduous, will immediately commence making young rootlets and will continue to do so more or less during the winter; particularly if a mulch has been placed around the base of the trees to protect them from deep soil frost. During the fall period there is very little loss of water through transpiration since there are no leaves; so the sap of the tree will furnish sufficient food material for root growth.

HOW NEW ROOT-HAIRS ARE FORMED ON TRANSPLANTED STOCK

If the feeding root-hairs are destroyed or injured in transplanting, new ones will have to be produced before the plant can make any healthy growth. Thus, this is the critical time for transplanted stock. These new roots start from the cambium layer underneath the bark and develop most

[150]

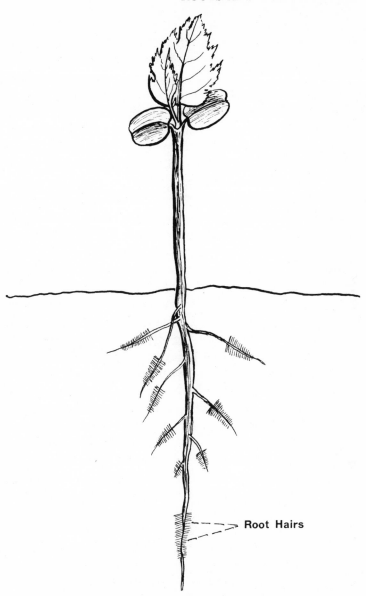

Root Hairs

Root hairs on transplanted stock

[151]

readily from younger roots. This reproduction of a new root system is very slow on older, thick roots, especially when they have already a strongly developed bark or when the soil temperature is too low or when there is not enough moisture in the soil. Growth of the top slackens or shortens in proportion to the remaining root-hair system. That is why a transplanted plant often appears to be standing still for weeks. The root system of a transplanted tree or shrub or even of an herb is less able to supply its full complement of leaves with water than previous to its removal; the balance has been broken. Thus, judicious cutting back of the top of the tree or shrub (or even the leaf surface of an herb) is necessary in transplanting to assure success, since this enables the plant to develop a new root system. While this is taking place the few remaining roots have a chance to supply the decreased top material for transpiration and photosynthesis. If given half a chance, the root system will soon develop a balance for the top of the plant. Failure to observe this fact is one of the major reasons why an amateur so often has no success in transplanting; he simply will not cut back the top to balance the remaining root system. It is during the transplanting period that pruning of shrubs and trees is the most critical matter, particularly in the case of fruit trees. Since the transplanted plant must be topped to balance the remaining root system, one should cut out all faulty branches, remove branches to give shape to the plant, and if the plants are fruiting trees, the general form can then be made. The general rule is: reduce the aerial part in proportion to root destruction. Cutting back leaf surface to prevent excess evaporation gives the remaining rootlets a chance to take hold again and return to the natural balance of the root system to the aerial shoots and leaves.

[152]

APPENDIX

PRUNING GUIDE FOR 225 WOODY ORNAMENTALS

Latin Name	Common Name	Kind and Mature Size	Duration of Foliage*	Why Prune	How Much to Cut	When to Prune
Abelia		Shrub 3-6 ft.	E	To promote bushy growth; to repair	Remove deadwood, thin once in 3 or 4 years	As new growth starts
Abies	Fir	Tree to 100 ft.	E	Shape when young	Enough to correct branching	June and July
Acacia farnesiana	Opopanax	Shrub to 12 ft.	E	To control spread	As needed	After blooming
Acanthopanax	Five-leaved aralia	Shrub 10-15 ft.	D	Repair	Deadwood	While dormant
Acer	Maple	Trees to 100 ft.	D	Corrective	Only as needed	Midsummer
Actinidia	Silver vine	Vine to 50 ft.	D	Repair, training	As needed	While dormant
Aesculus	Horse chestnut, Buckeye	Shrub 6-10 ft. or tree 60 ft.	D	Repair	Little as possible	After blooming
Ailanthus		Tree to 60 ft.	D		None	
Akebia		Slender vine	D		Little	After blooming
Allamanda neriifolia	Allamanda	6 ft. shrub	E	Seldom needed	Little	After blooming
Amelanchier	Juneberry, Shadblow	Tree or shrub, various	E	Repair	Remove deadwood	After blooming
Amorpha fruticosa	False indigo	Shrub 10-15 ft.	D	Stimulate growth	Remove all 2-yr. wood, all 1-yr. back to few buds	While dormant
Ampelopsis heterophylla		Slender vine	D		Little	After blooming
Andromeda	Bog rosemary	Shrub 1-3 ft.	E	Repair	Remove dead flowers	March to June

*E—evergreen or evergrowing; S—semi-evergreen; D—deciduous

[153]

PRUNING GUIDE FOR 225 WOODY ORNAMENTALS (Continued)

Latin Name	Common Name	Kind and Mature Size	Duration of Foliage*	Why Prune	How Much to Cut	When to Prune
Aralia	Angelica tree	Tree to 40 ft.	D	Repair	Deadwood	Spring
Arbutus	Madrona, strawberry tree	20-ft. shrub	E	Shaping	Little as possible	After blooming
Archontophoenix alexandrae	King palm, Alexander palm	Tree to 50 ft.	E		None	
Arctostaphylos	Bearberry	Prostrate	E		None	
Arecastrum romanzoffianum	Queenpalm	Tree to 35 ft.	E		None	
Aristolochia	Dutchman's-pipe	Vine to 50 ft.	D	Rampant, may need restraint	As needed	After blooming
Aronia	Chokeberry	Shrub 3-6 ft.	D		Thrives under neglect	
Artemisia	Wormwood	Shrub 3-6 ft.	D	Control size and shape	Remove all old wood and 1/2 to 3/4 of new wood	Late winter
Baccharis halimifolia	Groundsel shrub	Shrub 6-10 ft.	S	Repair	Old fruit clusters	While dormant
Bambusa	Bamboo	Woody 3-15 ft. grasses	D	To stimulate new growth	Thin out old shoots to ground. Root-prune for hedge	As growth starts
Bauhinia acuminata	Bauhinia	Shrub to 6 ft.	D, E	To keep compact form	Invasive branches	Late winter
Benzoin aestivale	Spice bush	Shrub 6-10 ft.	D	None	Thrives under neglect	

*E—evergreen or evergrowing; S—semi-evergreen; D—deciduous

PRUNING GUIDE FOR 225 WOODY ORNAMENTALS (Continued)

Latin Name	Common Name	Kind and Mature Size	Duration of Foliage*	Why Prune	How Much to Cut	When to Prune
Berberis	Barberry	Shrubs, various	D, E	To shape	Remove all 3-yr. wood each year, or cut to ground every 5-7 yrs.	Shape in winter, mid-summer
Betula	Birch	Tree to 60 ft.	D	Remove deadwood	As necessary	Summer only
Bismarckia nobilis	Bismarck's palm	Tree to 50 ft.	E		None	
Bougainvillea		Vine to 20 ft.	E		None	
Brunfelsia	Yesterday, today and tomorrow	Shrub 3-5 ft.	E	Shape	As needed	Summer
Buddleia davidi	Butterfly bush	Shrub 3-6 ft.	D	To promote heavier bloom	To 12 inches annually, and thin new shoots	Early spring and before blooming
Buxus	Box	Shrub, various	E	Repair, to shape if hedge	As necessary	As growth starts
Callicarpa	Beauty-berry	Shrub 1-3 ft.	D	Repair	Winter injury may need heavy cutting. Thin.	Early spring
Calluna vulgaris	Scotch heather	Shrub 1-3 ft.	E	To stimulate growth	Cut back severely	Early spring
Calycanthus floridus	Sweet shrub	Shrub 3-6 ft.	D	Repair	Deadwood only	After flowering
Camellia		Trees and shrubs, various	E	Repair, disbud for exhibition flowers	Remove old flowers, thin twiggy growth	After heavy flowering
Campsis radicans	Trumpet creeper	Vine to 50 ft.	D	To control	Cut back rampant new growth	Summer
Caragana	Pea shrub	Shrub 10-15 ft.	D	Repair	Remove deadwood	After blooming
Carya	Hickory	Trees to 100 ft.	D	To shape	As necessary while young	Summer

*E—evergreen or evergrowing; S—semi-evergreen; D—deciduous

Latin Name	Common Name	Kind and Mature Size	Duration of Foliage*	Why Prune	How Much to Cut	When to Prune
Caryopteris	Bluebeard	Shrub 1-3 ft.	D	Promote bushiness	Every year cut back to 6 inches	As growth starts
Cassia bicap-sularis	Cassia	Shrub 8-10 ft.	E	For compact growth	Cut back new growth	Early spring
Castanea	Chestnut	Tree to 100 ft.	D	To shape when young	As needed	Summer
Catalpa	Catalpa	Tree to 100 ft.	D	Shape when young	As needed	While dormant
Ceanothus	Jersey tea	Shrub 3-6 ft.	D	Flowering species, to stimulate bloom; foliage species to keep center open	Flowering—cut back to a few buds Foliage—as necessary	While dormant
Cedrus	Cedar	Tree to 100 ft.	E	To shape	Cut back green wood only	Spring to midsummer
Celastrus orbicu-latus	Bittersweet	Vine to 50 ft.	D	If crowded	Thin	Early spring
Cephalanthus occidentalis	Buttonbush	Shrub 3-6 ft.	D	To shape	As needed	Early spring
Cercis	Redbud, Judas tree	Tree to 20 ft.	D	Repair, shape while young	Deadwood	After blooming
Chaenomeles lagenaria	Flowering quince	Shrub to 10 ft.	D	Repair, to control size	Cut back new growth	After blooming
Chamaecyparis ericoides	False cypress	Shrub 10-15 ft., dwarf, 1-3 ft.	E	To shape	Little as possible	Midsummer
Chamaedaphne	Leatherleaf	Shrub 1-3 ft.	S		Little as possible	After blooming
Chamaerops humilis	European fan palm	Tree to 15 ft.	E	To remove or restrain sucker growth	As needed	Any time

*E—evergreen or evergrowing; S—semi-evergreen; D—deciduous

PRUNING GUIDE FOR 225 WOODY ORNAMENTALS (Continued)

Latin Name	Common Name	Kind and Mature Size	Duration of Foliage*	Why Prune	How Much to Cut	When to Prune
Chilopsis	Desert willow	Shrubby tree to 20 ft.	D		None	
Chimonanthes praecox	Wintersweet	Shrub to 10 ft.	D		None	
Chionanthus virginica	White fringe tree	Tree to 20 ft.	D	Repair	Deadwood	After blooming
Cinnamomum camphora	Camphor tree	Tree to 40 ft.	E	Repair	As needed. Do not compost trimmings	Summer
Cistus	Rock rose	Shrub, 2-8 ft.	S	Only to remove old flowers	None	After blooming
Cladrastis lutea	Yellow wood	Tree to 40 ft.	D	Repair		After blooming
Clematis		Vines to 20 ft.	D	Tops may winterkill	Cut back to green cambium if winterkilled	Before growth starts
Clerodendron	Glory bower	Shrub 6-10 ft.	D	Neatness	Some species need none; C. speciosissimum cut to ground	Early spring
Clethra alnifolia	Summersweet	Shrub 3-6 ft.	D	Repair	Little as possible	Early spring
Cneorum	Spurge olive	Shrub, 4 ft.	E		None	
Cocos nucifera	Coconut	Tree to 75 ft.	E		None	
Colutea	Bladder senna	Shrub 6-15 ft.	D	Repair, to control size	Remove most of previous year's growth; remove old flower stems	While dormant and midsummer

*E—evergreen or evergrowing; S—semi-evergreen; D—deciduous

[157]

PRUNING GUIDE FOR 225 WOODY ORNAMENTALS (Continued)

Latin Name	Common Name	Kind and Mature Size	Duration of Foliage*	Why Prune	How Much to Cut	When to Prune
Cornus	Dogwood	Shrubs, various	D	For control, for colored stems	Cut to ground	Early spring
Cornus florida	Flowering dogwood	Tree to 20 ft.	D	Corrective only	Very little	After blooming
Corylopsis	Winter hazel	Shrub 1-3 ft.	D		None	
Cotoneaster horizontalis	Spreading cotoneaster	Shrub—low	D	To control size and shape; to repair	Part of new growth, if necessary	Early spring
Crataegus	Hawthorn	Shrub or tree to 25 ft.	D	Corrective	Little as possible	After blooming
Cydonia	Japanese quince	Tree to 20 ft.	D	If used as hedge, to shape	If used as tree, none	After blooming
Cyrilla racemiflora	Titi	Tree or shrub to 20 ft.	E	To increase bloom	As needed	After blooming
Cytisus	Broom	Shrub 1-6 ft.	S	Repair and shape	Deadwood and some new wood	After blooming
Daphne cneorum	Garland flower	Shrub 1-3 ft.	E	To shape and maintain bushiness	Head back	After blooming
Delonix regia	Royal poinciana	Tree to 25 ft.	D	Repair	As needed	After heaviest blooming
Deutzia		Shrub 3-10 ft.	D	Renewal	Remove some old canes each year	After blooming
Dictyosperma alba	Princess palm	Tree to 30 ft.	E		None	
Diervilla canadensis		Shrub 3-10 ft.	D	General tidiness	Cut back new wood after blooming; remove old wood	After blooming Late winter

*E—evergreen or evergrowing; S—semi-evergreen; D—deciduous

Latin Name	Common Name	Kind and Mature Size	Duration of Foliage*	Why Prune	How Much to Cut	When to Prune
Dirca palustris	Leatherwood	Shrub 3-6 ft.	D	Repair	Little as possible	After blooming
Elaeagnus	Oleaster, wild olive	Shrub 6-20 ft.	D	None	Likes neglect	
Enkianthus		Shrub 3-10 ft.	D		None	
Erica	Heath	Shrubs or trees, various	E	Repair; remove faded flowers	Little as possible	After blooming
Ervatamia coronaria	Crape jasmine	Shrub to 6 ft.	D		As little as possible	
Escallonia		Shrub, various	D	To shape, if hedge	As needed	After blooming
Eucalyptus pulverulenta	Eucalyptus	Tree to 15 ft.	E	To increase branching	Thin when young	Any time
Euonymus	Spindle tree, strawberry bush	Slender vine or shrub, various sizes	E, D	To control size and shape	Thin occasionally	Midsummer
Euphorbia pulcherrima	Poinsettia	Shrub 4-8 ft.	E		None	
Exochorda	Pearl bush	Shrub 6-10 ft.	D	To shape	As needed	After blooming
Fagus	Beech	Tree to 100 ft.	D	If shade is too dense	Thin branches	Summer
Ficus benjamina	Weeping fig	Tree to 30 ft.	E	To shape	Thin occasionally	February
Forsythia	Goldenbells	Shrub 6-10 ft.	D	To increase flowering	Remove all 2- and 3-year wood	Immediately after blooming
Fothergilla		Shrub 3-10 ft.	D		None	

*E—evergreen or evergrowing; S—semi-evergreen; D—deciduous

[159]

PRUNING GUIDE FOR 225 WOODY ORNAMENTALS (Continued)

Latin Name	Common Name	Kind and Mature Size	Duration of Foliage*	Why Prune	How Much to Cut	When to Prune
Fremontia californica	Flannel bush	Shrub to 10 ft.	E	Shape	Cut back longest branches	Spring
Fuchsia		Shrubs or trees to 18 ft.	E	Shape and repair	Cut back young branches to 2 buds	February
Gardenia jasminoides	Cape jasmine	Shrub, 6 ft.	E		Only to cut flowers	
Gaultheria	Wintergreen	Low shrub	E		None	
Gaylussacia	Black huckleberry	Shrub 1-6 ft.	E	Repair	Little as possible	After blooming
Gelsemium sempervirens	Carolina jessamine	Vine to 20 ft.	E		None	
Genista	Rock broom	Shrub 1-3 ft.	E	To stimulate growth	Cut to ground	Late winter
Ginkgo biloba	Maidenhair tree	Tree to 60 ft.	D		None	
Gleditsia	Honey locust	Tree to 60 ft.	D		None	
Gordonia	Loblolly bay	Tree to 20 ft.	E		None	
Halesia	Silver bell	Shrub or tree to 60 ft.	D	To shape	Thin occasionally	After blooming
Hamamelis	Witch hazel	Tree-like shrub 10-30 ft.	D	Repair, shape when young	Little as possible	After blooming
Hedera	Ivy	Vine to 20 ft.	E	Shape, if grown as bush	If allowed to climb, cut close to wall. In summer, remove long shoots	Early spring, also midsummer
Helianthemum	Sun rose	Ground cover	S	Repair	Remove faded flowers	After blooming

*E—evergreen or evergrowing; S—semi-evergreen; D—deciduous

PRUNING GUIDE FOR 225 WOODY ORNAMENTALS (Continued)

Latin Name	Common Name	Kind and Mature Size	Duration of Foliage*	Why Prune	How Much to Cut	When to Prune
Hibiscus syriacus	Rose of Sharon	Shrub, 15 ft.	D	Increase flower size	Thin out smaller branches	Early spring
Hippophae rhamnoides	Sea buckthorn	Tree to 40 ft.	S	Repair	As needed	After blooming
Hydrangea		Shrub 3-10 ft.	D	Improve bloom	Cut to ground every year	Early spring
Hypericum	St. John's-wort	Shrub 1-6 ft.	D	Repair and renewal	Thin old wood; remove seed pods and deadwood	While dormant
Ilex	Holly, inkberry	Tree-like shrub 6-15 ft.	E	To shape, if necessary	Remove some laterals if desired, but cut little	June or July
Indigofera	Indigo	Shrub various	D	Promote bushiness and flowering	Remove all 2-year wood; cut back 1-yr. wood	While dormant
Itea virginica	Sweet spire	Shrub 1-3 ft.	D	Shape	Thin old shoots and shorten young ones	February
Jacaranda		Tree to 50 ft.	D	Repair	Cut dead, weak branches	When needed
Jasminum	Jasmine	Shrub 5-15 ft.	E	To shape and encourage flowering	Occasionally thin and head back	After blooming
Jubaea spectabilis	Chilean wine palm	Tree to 60 ft.	E		None	
Juglans	Walnut	Tree to 100 ft.	D		None	
Juniperus	Juniper	Tree-like shrub, or trailing	E	To control shape and size	Up to ½ of new growth	June or July, also September
Kalmia latifolia	Mountain laurel	Shrub 10-15 ft.	E	Remove spent flowers	Little as possible	Fall or winter
Kerria japonica	Kerrybush	Shrub 1-6 ft.	D	Repair or renewal	Occasionally cut back some old branches to ground	Early spring

*E—evergreen or evergrowing; S—semi-evergreen; D—deciduous

[161]

PRUNING GUIDE FOR 225 WOODY ORNAMENTALS (Continued)

Latin Name	Common Name	Kind and Mature Size	Duration of Foliage*	Why Prune	How Much to Cut	When to Prune
Koelreuteria paniculata	Varnish tree, golden rain tree	Tree to 40 ft.	D	Repair	As needed	Early spring
Kolkwitzia amabilis	Beauty bush	Shrub 3-6 ft.	D	To prevent legginess	A few of oldest canes annually	After blooming
Laburnum	Golden chain	Tree-like shrub to 25 ft.	D	Repair	Little as possible	After blooming
Lagerstroemia speciosa	Crape myrtle	Shrub to 20 ft.	D	To encourage new growth	Cut back most vigorous shoots	After blooming
Lantana montevidensis	Lantana	Ground cover, 1 ft.	E		None	
Larix	Larch	Tree to 100 ft.	D		None	
Laurus nobilis	Sweet bay	Tree to 40 ft.	E	Shaping	Clip tub plants 2 to 3 times	Summer
Lavandula	Lavender	Shrub to 3 ft.	E		None. Cutting flowers sufficient	
Ledum	Wild rosemary	Shrub 1-3 ft.	E		None	
Leiophyllum buxifolium	Sand myrtle	Shrub 1-3 ft.	E	Repair	As needed	After blooming
Lespedeza bicolor	Bush clover	Shrub 3-10 ft.	D	Neatness	Cut back moderately	While dormant
Leucophyllum texanum	Barometer bush	Shrub to 8 ft.	E	To shape	Cut back if used as hedge	Winter
Leucothoe catesbi	Drooping leucothoe	Shrub 3-6 ft.	E	Renewal. Remove spent flowers	Remove canes weakened by age	After blooming

*E—evergreen or evergrowing; S—semi-evergreen; D—deciduous

PRUNING GUIDE FOR 225 WOODY ORNAMENTALS (Continued)

Latin Name	Common Name	Kind and Mature Size	Duration of Foliage*	Why Prune	How Much to Cut	When to Prune
Licuala grandis	Licuala	Tree to 6 ft.	E	Repair	As needed	Any time
Ligustrum	Privet	Shrub, various	S	To shape	Several shearings of 4 to 6 in. of new growth	Summer
Liquidambar styraciflua	Sweet gum	Tree to 60 ft.	D		Very little	
Liriodendron tulipifera	Tulip tree	Tree to 200 ft.	D		None	
Lonicera fragrantissima	Honeysuckle	Vine 6-10 ft.	S	Repair	Deadwood only	After blooming
Loropetalum chinense	Loropetalum	Shrub 10 ft.	E	To keep it low and spreading	Part of new growth	After blooming
Lycium	Matrimony vine	Vine 6-10 ft.	S	None	Likes neglect	
Lyonia		Shrub 6-10 ft.			None	
Magnolia		Tree to 60 ft.	D	Corrective, to shape	As little as possible	After blooming, except M. glauca
Mahonia	Oregon holly-grape	Shrub 1-6 ft.	E	Repair, to maintain size	If grown as ground cover, shorten each year	Midsummer
Menispermum	Moonseed	Vine	D	Shape	Remove ragged growth	Late winter
Michelia fuscata	Banana shrub	Shrub to 15 ft.	E		Very little	After blooming
Myrica	Bayberry	Shrub 3-10 ft.	S	Corrective	Very little, to preserve berries	After blooming
Myrtus	Myrtle	Shrub 3-9 ft.	E	To shape, if near wall	Cut back	March

*E—evergreen or evergrowing; S—semi-evergreen; D—deciduous

PRUNING GUIDE FOR 225 WOODY ORNAMENTALS (Continued)

Latin Name	Common Name	Kind and Mature Size	Duration of Foliage*	Why Prune	How Much to Cut	When to Prune
Nandina domestica	Heavenly bamboo	Shrub 6-8 ft.	E	To promote suckering	Remove oldest canes	As growth starts
Nemopanthus mucronata	Mountain holly	Shrub 6-10 ft.	D		Little as possible	After blooming
Nerium oleander	Oleander	Shrub to 12 ft.	E	Repair only	As necessary	After blooming
Nyssa sylvatica biflora	Tupelo	Tree to 60 ft.	D	Shaping, when young	As needed	Summer
Osmanthus fragrans	Sweet olive	Shrub 8 ft.	E	If overgrown	Cut back sharply	Any time
Oxydendrum arboreum	Sorrel tree, sourwood	Tree to 30 ft.	D	Repair	As needed	After blooming
Pachysandra		Ground cover	E		None	
Paeonia suffruticosa	Tree peony	Shrub 4-6 ft.	D	Repair	Tips of branches die off—remove	While dormant
Parthenocissus	Virginia creeper, Japanese and Boston ivy	Vine to 50 ft.	D	Repair	Cut to ground when planted to help shoots start to climb	Summer
Passiflora caerulea	Passionflower	Vine to 20 ft.	E	To renew	Cut back secondary branches to few buds	Late winter
Paulownia tomentosa	Royal paulownia	Tree to 35 ft.	D	Repair	As needed	Summer
Paurotis wrighti	Paurotis	Tree to 35 ft.	E	Repair	As needed	Anytime

*E—evergreen or evergrowing; S—semi-evergreen; D—deciduous

PRUNING GUIDE FOR 225 WOODY ORNAMENTALS (Continued)

Latin Name	Common Name	Kind and Mature Size	Duration of Foliage*	Why Prune	How Much to Cut	When to Prune
Philadelphus	Mock orange	Shrub, various	D	Remove flowers, shape	Cut back unwanted growth	After blooming
Philodendron		Shrub 4-5 ft.	E	Repair	Remove winter injury	Summer
Physocarpus opulifolius	Ninebark	Shrub 10 ft.	D	To encourage flowering	Cut back	Summer
Picea	Spruce	Tree to 100 ft.	E		None	
Pieris	Fetterbush	Shrub 3-6 ft.	E	Repair	Little as possible	After blooming
Pinus	Pine	Tree to 100 ft.	E	Repair	Remove deadwood only	Midsummer
Pittosporum	Australian laurel	Shrub 10 ft.	E	Repair	As needed	Any time
Platanus	Sycamore	Tree to 100 ft.	D		None	
Plumbago capensis	Plumbago	Shrub 2-8 ft.	E		None	
Poinciana gilliesi	Bird-of-paradise bush	Shrub 12 ft.	D	To shape	As needed	Late winter
Populus nigra italica	Lombardy poplar	Tree to 100 ft.	D	Corrective only	As needed	Spring or summer
Potentilla	Cinquefoil	Shrub 1-3 ft.	D	None	Likes neglect	
Pritchardia pacifica	Fiji fan palm	Tree to 30 ft.	E		None	
Prunus	Flowering almond, cherry	Tree or shrub, various	D	To shape	Occasionally thin out old shrub stems	After blooming
Pyracantha	Firethorn	Shrub 6-10 ft.	D	Heavier berrying	In winter, cut back wood that fruited; pinch back new growth in summer	

*E—evergreen or evergrowing; S—semi-evergreen; D—deciduous

[165]

PRUNING GUIDE FOR 225 WOODY ORNAMENTALS (Continued)

Latin Name	Common Name	Kind and Mature Size	Duration of Foliage*	Why Prune	How Much to Cut	When to Prune
Pyrus (and Malus)	Flowering crab	Tree to 40 ft.	D	To thicken plant	Half of new growth in young tree	June and July
Quercus	Oak	Tree, 100 ft.	D		None	
Raphiolepsis indica	India hawthorn	Shrub 5 ft.	E		Little as possible	After blooming
Rhododendron (and Azalea)		Shrubs, various	E, D	Remove old flowers to maintain size	Very little	June
Rhodotypos	Jetbead White kerria	Shrub 3-6 ft.	D	Shaping	Little as possible, to pre- serve berries	After blooming
Rhus	Smoke tree Sumac	Tree-like shrub over 15 ft.	D	Stimulate growth, repair	Cut out 2-yr. wood and 1- yr. back to few eyes	Early spring
Ribes	Flowering currant	Shrub 3-10 ft.	D	Repair	Little as possible	After blooming
Robinia hispida	Rose acacia	Shrub 3-6 ft.	D	Repair, remove suckers	As needed	After blooming
Rosa	Bush roses	Shrub 6-10 ft.	D	Renewal	When overgrown, remove oldest canes	After blooming
Rosa	Small flower climbers	Vine to 20 ft.	D	To rejuvenate	Flowers and all old wood	After blooming
Rosa	Everblooming	Shrub 3-6 ft.	D	For bloom	Teas to 8-12 in. Floribundas to 12-15 in. Grandifloras to 18-24 in.	After new growth starts
Rosmarinus officinalis	Rosemary	Shrub to 6 ft.	E	For cookery	Cutting herb for culinary use sufficient	Before blooming
Roystonea regia	Royal palm	Tree to 80 ft.	E		None	

*E—evergreen or evergrowing; S—semi-evergreen; D—deciduous

PRUNING GUIDE FOR 225 WOODY ORNAMENTALS (Continued)

Latin Name	Common Name	Kind and Mature Size	Duration of Foliage*	Why Prune	How Much to Cut	When to Prune
Rubus odorata	Flowering rasp-berry	Shrub 3-6 ft.	D	To increase bloom, prevent spreading	Remove old canes and pinch back growing tips	After blooming
Sabal palmetto	Cabbage palm	Tree to 60 ft.	E		Tree dies if terminal bud removed	
Salix	Willow	Shrub or tree, various	D	Corrective only	As needed	Any time
Sambucus canadensis	American elder	Tree-like shrub 10-15 ft.	D	To control size	As needed	Late winter
Sassafras albidum	Sassafras	Tree to 60 ft.	D	To maintain tree shape	Remove suckers	Late winter
Serissa foetida	Serissa	Shrub 3 ft.	E	To shape	As needed	After blooming
Shepherdia argentea	Buffalo berry	Shrub 10-15 ft.	D	To prevent legginess	Cut back longest shoots	Summer
Skimmia japonica	Skimmia	Shrub 4 ft.	E		Little or none	
Smilax	Greenbrier, cat-brier	Vine	E, D	To control	Thin and cut back to prevent forming thicket	While dormant
Sophora japonica	Scholar tree	Tree to 60 ft.	D		None	
Sorbaria	False spirea	Shrub 6-15 ft.	D	Shape	Prune heavily	While dormant
Spiraea	Bumalda, Douglasi, Anthony Waterer	Shrubs, various	D	To promote flowering	Remove all old stems and ½ new growth	Early spring
Spiraea	Van Houtte			To shape		After blooming
Staphylea	Bladdernut	Shrub 6-10 ft.	D	Repair	Deadwood	Early spring

*E—evergreen or evergrowing; S—semi-evergreen; D—deciduous

[167]

Latin Name	Common Name	Kind and Mature Size	Duration of Foliage*	Why Prune	How Much to Cut	When to Prune
Stephanandra incisa	Cut-leaf stephanandra	Shrub 3-6 ft.	D	Repair	Remove seed pods, old wood	While dormant
Stewartia pseudocamellia		Tree to 40 ft.	D	Repair		While dormant
Styrax japonica	Storax	Tree or shrub 20-30 ft.	D	To shape	As needed	After blooming
Symphoricarpos	Snowberry, coral berry	Shrub 3-6 ft.	D	Repair, to stimulate new growth	Remove all 2-yr. wood and 1-yr. back to 2 eyes	Early spring
Symplocos crataegoides		Shrub over 15 ft.	E	Repair		After blooming
Syringa	Lilac	Shrub to 15 ft.	D	Remove old flowers and suckers	As little as possible	After blooming
Tamarix	Tamarisk	Tree-like shrub 6-15 ft.	D, E	Promote flowering	Cut back severely	After blooming
Taxus cuspidata	Yew	Trees or shrubs	E	To maintain size or shape	To ½ new growth	June or July
Tecomaria capensis	Cape honeysuckle	Shrub 3-10 ft.	E	To control size	Thin and head back new growth often	Any time
Thea sinensis	Tea	Shrub 10 ft.	E	Shape	As needed	After blooming
Thrinax parviflora	Florida thatch palm	Tree to 25 ft.	E		None	
Thuja	Arbor vitae	Trees, various	E	To control size and shape	Slight	Late June or July
Tilia	Linden	Tree to 100 ft.	D		None	

*E—evergreen or evergrowing; S—semi-evergreen; D—deciduous

PRUNING GUIDE FOR 225 WOODY ORNAMENTALS (Continued)

Latin Name	Common Name	Kind and Mature Size	Duration of Foliage*	Why Prune	How Much to Cut	When to Prune
Trachycarpus fortunei	Windmill palm	Tree to 40 ft.	E		None	
Tsuga	Hemlock	Tree to 100 ft.	E	To shape and thicken	Up to ½ new growth	June, July, or Sept.
Ulmus americana	American elm	Tree to 100 ft.	D	Corrective only	As needed, but useless to try to eliminate weak crotches	Summer
Vaccinium	Highbush or lowbush blueberry	Shrub 10-15 or 1-3 ft. resp.	E		Little	After blooming
Veitchia merrilli	Christmas palm	Tree, to 20 ft.	E	To remove dead leaves		Any time
Viburnum	Highbush cranberry, snowball	Shrub, various	D	To maintain size	As needed. V. Carlesi, cut 3-yr. wood to ground	After blooming
Vinca	Periwinkle	Ground cover	E		None	
Vitex agnus-castus	Chaste tree	Shrub 6-10 ft.	D	Remove dead or weak growth	Back to vigorous bud	Early spring
Washingtonia robusta	Washingtonia	Tree to 80 ft.	E	Appearance	Remove dead fronds if possible	Any time
Weigela		Shrub 6-10 ft.	D	To control size and shape	Cut back ½ new growth	Midsummer
Wisteria		Vine to 50 ft., plus	D	Promote flowering	Heavy heading back of new growth	Midsummer
Yucca filamentosa	Yucca	Shrub to 8 ft.	E		None	
Zenobia pulverulenta		Shrub 3-6 ft.	S	Repair	As needed	Summer

*E—evergreen or evergrowing; S—semi-evergreen; D—deciduous.

[169]

INDEX

[171]

INDEX

INDEX

INDEX

[176]